ASIAN SNACKS

ASIAN SNACKS

Over 50 recipes for crunchy, spicy and umami-rich bites

RYLAND PETERS & SMALL

Designer Paul Stradling
Editor Abi Waters
Production Manager Gordana Simakovic
Creative Director Leslie Harrington
Editorial Director Julia Charles

Indexer Vanessa Bird

Published in 2025 by Ryland Peters & Small
20–21 Jockey's Fields
London WC1R 4BW
and
1452 Davis Bugg Road,
Warrenton, NC 27589

www.rylandpeters.com
email: euregulations@rylandpeters.com

Text © Ghillie Başan, Jordan Bourke, James Campbell, Ross Dobson, Matt Follas, Dunja Gulin, Tori Haschka, Carol Hilker, Vicky Jones, Jackie Kearney, Jenny Linford, Loretta Liu, Uyen Luu, Nitisha Patel, Louise Pickford, Annie Rigg, Fiona Smith and Ryland Peters & Small 2025. Design and photography © Ryland Peters & Small 2025. (See page 128 for full credits.)

ISBN: 978-1-78879-722-1

10 9 8 7 6 5 4 3 2 1

The authors' moral rights have been asserted. All rights reserved. No part of this publication may be reproduced, stored in a retrieval system or transmitted in any form or by any means, electronic, mechanical, photocopying or otherwise, without the prior permission of the publisher.

A CIP record for this book is available from the British Library.
US Library of Congress Cataloging-in-Publication data has been applied for.

The authorised representative in the EEA is Authorised Rep Compliance Ltd., Ground Floor, 71 Lower Baggot Street, Dublin, D02 P593, Ireland
www.arccompliance.com

Printed and bound in China.

NOTES

• Both British (Metric) and American (Imperial ounces plus US cups) are included in these recipes for your convenience; however, it is important to work with one set of measurements only and not alternate between the two within a recipe.

• All spoon measurements are level unless otherwise specified.

• All eggs are medium (UK) or large (US), unless specified as large, in which case US extra-large should be used. Uncooked or partially cooked eggs should not be served to the very old, frail, young children, pregnant women or those with compromised immune systems.

• Ovens should be preheated to the specified temperatures. We recommend using an oven thermometer. If using a fan-assisted oven, adjust temperatures according to the manufacturer's instructions.

• When a recipe calls for the grated zest of citrus fruit, buy unwaxed fruit and wash well before using. If you can only find treated fruit, scrub well in warm soapy water before using.

CONTENTS

INTRODUCTION	7
DOUGH RECIPES FOR BAO & DUMPLINGS	8
VINEGARED RICE	9
DIPPING SAUCES	10
SUSHI & SASHIMI	12
BUNS & DUMPLINGS	26
ROLLS & PANCAKES	48
FRITTERS & FRIED SNACKS	70
SKEWERS & WINGS	92
SWEET THINGS	108
INDEX	126
CREDITS	128

INTRODUCTION

Immerse yourself in the delicious world of Asian snacks with this fantastic collection of over 50 recipes, from samosas to sushi and dumplings to dosa.

Food from Eastern corners of the world is often thought of as some of the most exciting and enticing on the planet. Whether umami-rich with Japanese miso or soy sauce, spiked with gently building layers of aromatic Indian spices, or replete with fragrant Thai herbs, chilli and garlic, each mouthful packs a big flavour punch.

The savoury bites that usually serve as a precursor to an Asian meal are no exception flavour-wise. Snacks from street-food markets around Asia have also become increasingly popular in recent times, fuelling our appetite for these irresistible snacks.

This book enables you to travel around the Far East from the comfort of your own home and discover the vast array of popular small bites that are on offer. Pick from Chinese spring rolls, Indonesian satay skewers, Japanese yakitori chicken, Korean bulgogi wraps, Vietnamese summer rolls, Indian dhal fritters and a whole host more to choose from.

These wide-ranging recipes will satisfy any craving. Whether it's a crispy fried fritter or pancake, a succulent and rich skewer or chicken wing, fresh and simple sushi, or unctuous bao buns filled with spiced meat or vegetable mixtures. Why not choose several recipes from around Asia to create an enticing pan-Asian feast to share with family and friends.

It's not just savoury snacks that make an appearance. Sweet snacks from around Asia also feature and pair perfectly with the other savoury dishes if you are looking for a sweet hit to enjoy after your selection of Asian snacks..

Dive in and enjoy a great collection of delicious recipes that will satisfy any Asian-food aficionado's cravings.

DOUGH RECIPES FOR BAO & DUMPLINGS

EGG DOUGH

150 g/1 cup plus 2 tbsp Asian white wheat flour

40 ml/3 tbsp water

1 egg

MAKES 16 DUMPLING SKINS

Place the flour in a mixing bowl and add the water and egg. Mix together, then turn the dough out onto a lightly floured surface. Using lightly floured hands, knead for 20–25 minutes. The dough will be sticky at first but will become smooth and silky. Separate in half and roll into two equal cylinders, each about 2.5 cm/1 inch in diameter. Cover with a damp kitchen cloth and set aside to rest at room temperature for 30 minutes.

Use a sharp knife to slice the dough cylinders into 16 equal pieces. On a lightly floured surface, roll out each piece with a rolling pin until it has a neat round shape and a diameter of around 7.5 cm/3 inches.

FLUFFY BREAD DOUGH

230 g/1¾ cups plain/all-purpose flour

3 teaspoons baking powder

2 tablespoons caster/superfine sugar

80 ml/⅓ cup milk

3 tablespoons groundnut/peanut oil

salt

MAKES 24 DUMPLING SKINS

Put the flour in a large bowl and mix in the baking powder, sugar and ½ teaspoon salt.

Stir in the milk, oil and 70 ml/¼ cup plus 2 teaspoons water to form a dough.

Turn the dough onto a floured board and knead for 5 minutes until it becomes elastic.

Cover with clingfilm/plastic wrap and let it rest at room temperature for 1 hour.

BREAD DOUGH

2 tsp fast-action dried yeast

450 g/3½ cups Asian white wheat flour

100 g/¾ cup plus 1 tbsp icing/confectioners' sugar, sifted

15 g/2 tbsp dried milk powder

¼ tsp fine salt

2 tsp baking powder

180 ml/¾ cup water, add more if needed

50 ml/scant ¼ cup vegetable oil, plus extra for oiling

MAKES 16 BAO BUNS

Place the yeast in a large mixing bowl, then add the flour, sugar, milk powder, salt and baking powder. Make sure the yeast is separated from the salt by the layer of flour. Add the water and oil and bring together with a dough scraper. When no dry flour remains, remove the dough from the bowl and place on a lightly floured surface. Knead firmly for 5–10 minutes until smooth and elastic.

VINEGARED RICE

Sushi should never be put in the fridge (it will go hard). The vinegar in this rice will help preserve it for a few days if kept, wrapped, in a cool place.

400 ml/1¾ cups Japanese rice*

1 piece of dried kelp (kombu), 5 cm/2 inches square, for flavouring (optional)

3 tbsp Japanese rice vinegar

2½ tbsp sugar

2 tsp sea salt

MAKES 1 LITRE/4 CUPS

*Please note, the rice in this recipe is measured by volume, not weight.

Put the rice in a large bowl and wash it thoroughly, changing the water several times, until the water is clear. Drain and leave in the strainer for 1 hour. If short of time, soak the rice in clear cold water for 10–15 minutes, then drain.

Transfer to a deep, heavy-based saucepan, add 460 ml/2 cups water and a piece of dried kelp (kombu), if using. Cover and bring to the boil over a high heat for about 5 minutes. Discard the kelp. Lower the heat and simmer, covered, for about 10 minutes, or until all the water has been absorbed. Do not lift the lid. Remove from the heat and leave, still covered, for about 10–15 minutes.

Mix the rice vinegar, sugar and salt in a small jug/pitcher and stir until dissolved.

Transfer the cooked rice to a large, shallow dish or *handai* (Japanese wooden sumeshi tub). Sprinkle generously with the vinegar dressing. Using a wooden spatula, fold the vinegar dressing into the rice. Do not stir. While folding, cool the rice quickly using a fan. Let the rice cool to body temperature before using to make sushi.

Lightly oil the mixing bowl. Shape the dough into two cylinders and place back in the oiled bowl, cover with oiled cling film/plastic wrap and leave in a warm place to rise for 40–60 minutes or until doubled in size.

Remove the risen dough from the bowl, punch it down and knead it again briefly, but very carefully rather than firmly this time. Roll the dough out into a big rectangle and portion it out into 16 equal balls. Cover the dough balls with oiled cling film and leave to rest again for 30 minutes in a warm place.

Roll out each dough ball so that it has a diameter of around 7.5 cm/3 inches; try to make the centre slightly thicker than the edges so that it can hold the filling. Cover each dough circle with a damp kitchen cloth as you finish to stop it from drying out.

DIPPING SAUCES

CHINESE DIPPING SAUCE

A perfect sauce for steamed or fried wontons and all kinds of noodle dishes.

50 ml/scant ¼ cup light soy sauce
2 tsp Chinese black vinegar
1 tsp caster/granulated sugar
1 tsp fresh ginger, peeled and grated
1 tsp sesame oil
¼ tsp chilli/chile oil
sterilized glass jar with airtight lid
MAKES 75 ML/⅓ CUP

Whisk all the ingredients together in a bowl, or, if you have a clean glass jar with a lid, put all the ingredients into the jar, screw on the lid and shake well.

Serve immediately or store in a glass jar with an airtight lid in the fridge. The sauce will keep for up to 5 days.

JAPANESE DIPPING SAUCE

Traditionally served in hot summer months with chilled noodles.

200 ml/¾ cup dashi broth (see Note below)
3 tbsp Japanese soy sauce
3 tbsp mirin
½ tsp caster/granulated sugar
sterilized glass jar with airtight lid
MAKES 300 ML/1¼ CUPS

Whisk all the ingredients together in a bowl, or, in a clean glass jar with a lid and shake well.

Serve immediately or store in a glass jar with an airtight lid in the fridge. You can store the sauce in the fridge for up to 3 days.

Note: To make 1 litre/quart of dashi broth, pour 1.25 litres/1¼ quarts water into a pan, add 1 tablespoon chopped dried kombu and set aside for 30 minutes. Bring to the boil, removing any scum that appears on the surface, reduce the heat and simmer for 10 minutes. Remove the pan from the heat, stir in 1 tablespoon bonito flakes and let cool. Strain and use immediately or chill until required. The broth will keep stored in an airtight container for 3 days in the fridge or can be frozen for up to 1 month.

KOREAN DIPPING SAUCES

Korea is famed for its love of the condiment or side dish. Choganjang is the simplest of dipping sauces, perfect with all noodle dishes. Ssamjang is a spicy fermented chilli/chile bean paste, often served with Korean BBQ, but also delicious stirred into Korean soups. [Pictured on page 6]

CHOGANJANG

a pinch of sesame seeds
2 tbsp dark soy sauce
1 tbsp brown rice vinegar

MAKES 45 ML/3 TBSP

Dry-fry the sesame seeds in a small frying pan/skillet set over a medium heat until evenly toasted. Pour the soy sauce and vinegar into a small bowl and sprinkle with sesame seeds.

Use as required or store the soy and vinegar mixture without the sesame seeds in a sterilized glass bottle until ready to serve.

SSAMJANG

1 tsp sesame seeds
60 ml/¼ cup doenjang (Korean soy bean paste)
2 tsp gochujang (Korean chilli/chile paste)
1 spring onion/scallion, thinly sliced
1 small garlic clove, crushed/minced
1 Asian shallot, finely chopped
2 tsp rice wine
2 tsp sesame oil
1 tsp runny honey

MAKES 150 ML/⅔ CUP

Dry-fry the sesame seeds in a small frying pan/skillet set over a medium heat until evenly toasted. Put all the ingredients in a small bowl and use as required.

Alternatively, transfer to a plastic container, seal and store in the fridge for up to 3 days.

SUSHI & SASHIMI

WASABI MAYONNAISE & TUNA ROLL

This is a rather Western idea of sushi, but it is easy and convenient because it uses canned tuna, cutting out some of the fiddly preparation of fresh fish. Use Japanese mayonnaise if you can, but homemade or good-quality shop-bought mayonnaise works well.

4 sheets of nori seaweed

185 g/6½ oz. canned tuna in brine, drained

4 tsp Japanese or other mayonnaise

1 tsp wasabi paste, or to taste

125 g/4½ oz. baby corn, fresh or frozen, or equivalent drained canned baby corn

½ recipe vinegared rice (see page 9), divided into 4 portions

a sushi rolling mat

MAKES 24–28 PIECES

Put the tuna and mayonnaise in a bowl and stir in the wasabi paste.

If using fresh or frozen corn, bring a saucepan of water to the boil and cook the corn for 3 minutes, or until tender. Drain and rinse under cold water to cool. If using canned corn, drain and rinse.

Set a sheet of nori, rough side up, on a rolling mat with the long edge towards you. Top with 1 portion of the sushi rice, and spread it in a thin layer, leaving about 2 cm/¾ inch of bare nori on the far edge. Spoon a quarter of the tuna mixture in a line along the middle of the rice and top with a line of corn, set end to end.

Lift the edge of the mat closest to you and start rolling up the sushi away from you, pressing in the filling with your fingers as you roll. You may need a little water along the far edge to seal it. Repeat to make 4 rolls. Using a clean, wet knife, slice each roll into 6–7 even pieces.

PICKLED SALMON ROLL

Using pickled fish is a delicious compromise to the traditional raw fish used in sushi. It's very easy to pickle fish at home so do give this a go.

3 sheets of nori seaweed, halved

½ recipe vinegared rice (see page 9), divided into 6 portions

1 tsp wasabi paste (optional)

PICKLED SALMON

100 ml/⅔ cup rice wine vinegar

2 tsp salt

2 tbsp sugar

grated zest of 1 unwaxed lemon

300 g/10½ oz. salmon fillet, skinned and boned

4 shallots, finely sliced

a sushi rolling mat

MAKES 36–42 PIECES

To prepare the salmon, put the vinegar, salt, sugar and lemon zest in a saucepan with 60 ml/¼ cup water. Bring to the boil, reduce the heat, then simmer for 3 minutes. Let cool.

Put the salmon in a plastic container with the shallots. Pour the vinegar mixture over the top and cover tightly. Refrigerate for 2–3 days, turning the salmon in the pickle once a day.

When ready to make the sushi, drain the salmon and shallots. Slice the salmon as finely as possible and divide into 6 portions.

Put a half sheet of nori, rough side up, on a rolling mat with the long edge towards you. Top with 1 portion of the sushi rice and spread it out in a thin layer, leaving about 2 cm/¾ inch of bare nori at the far edge. Smear a little wasabi paste down the centre of the rice if you like. Arrange 1 portion of the salmon slices in a line along the middle of the rice and top with a line of the pickled shallots.

Lift the edge of the mat closest to you and start rolling the sushi away from you, pressing in the filling with your fingers as you roll. You may need a little water along the far edge to seal it. Repeat with the remaining ingredients to make 6 rolls. Using a clean wet knife, slice each roll into 6–7 even pieces.

MISO-MARINATED ASPARAGUS ROLL

Using just one simple ingredient can make a perfectly elegant filling for rolled sushi. Here, fresh green asparagus is marinated in white miso.

24 small or 12 medium asparagus spears

100 g/4 oz. white miso paste

2 tsp mirin (sweetened Japanese rice wine)

1 tsp wasabi paste

3 sheets of nori seaweed, halved

½ recipe vinegared rice (see page 9), divided into 6 portions

a sushi rolling mat

MAKES 36 PIECES

Snap off any tough ends of the asparagus and discard. Bring a large saucepan of water to the boil, add the asparagus spears and simmer for 3–4 minutes until tender. Drain, rinse in plenty of cold water, then let cool.

If using medium-sized asparagus spears, slice each piece in half lengthways to give 24 pieces in total. Arrange all the asparagus in a shallow dish.

Put the white miso paste, mirin and wasabi paste in a small bowl and mix well. Spread evenly over the asparagus and let marinate for 2–4 hours.

When ready to assemble the rolls, carefully scrape the marinade off the asparagus – it should be fairly clean so the miso doesn't overwhelm the flavour of the finished sushi.

Put 1 half-sheet of nori, rough side up, on the rolling mat. The long edge of the nori sheet should be towards you. Spread one portion of rice in a thin layer over the nori, leaving 2 cm/¾ inch bare on the far edge. Put 4 pieces of the asparagus in a line along the middle of the rice. Lift the edge of the mat closest to you and start rolling up the sushi away from you, pressing in the filling with your fingers as you roll. You may need a little water along the far edge to seal it. Repeat to make 6 rolls in all. Using a clean, wet knife, slice each roll into 6 even pieces and serve.

INSIDE-OUT AVOCADO ROLLS
WITH CHIVES & CASHEWS

Rolling inside-out sushi may seem a bit tricky, but it is actually very easy, because the rice on the outside moulds so well into shape.

2 small or 1 large ripe avocado

2 tsp fresh lemon juice

2 tbsp Japanese mayonnaise

¼ tsp salt

1 tsp wasabi paste (optional)

75 g/3 oz. cashew nuts, pan-toasted (roasted, salted cashews work well)

a small bunch of chives

2 sheets of nori seaweed, halved

½ recipe vinegared rice (see page 9)

a sushi rolling mat

MAKES 24 PIECES

Peel the avocado and cut the flesh into small chunks. Toss in a bowl with the lemon juice, mayonnaise, salt and wasabi, if using. Mash slightly as you toss but not until mushy. Divide into 4 portions.

Chop the cashew nuts very finely and put in a bowl. Chop the chives very finely and mix with the cashew nuts. Divide into 4 portions.

Put a sheet of cling film/plastic wrap on the rolling mat. Put half a sheet of nori on top, rough side up, with the long edge facing you. Divide the rice into 4 portions and spread 1 portion over the nori.

Sprinkle 1 portion of the nut and chive mixture on top of the rice. Press it in gently with your fingers.

Carefully lift the whole thing up and flip it over so the rice is face down on the cling film. Remove the sushi mat. Put one portion of the avocado in a line along the long edge of the nori closest to you. Carefully roll it up, cut in half, then cut each half into 3, giving 6 pieces. Repeat to make 4 rolls, giving 24 pieces.

SASHIMI & CUCUMBER BITES

600 g/1 lb. 5 oz. fresh or sashimi-grade fish (tuna is classic, but you can substitute any other sashimi-grade fish)

½ tsp white sugar

3 tbsp soy sauce

1 tbsp sesame oil

1 tbsp grated fresh ginger

1 tbsp finely chopped red chilli/chile

5 spring onions/scallions, chopped

1 tbsp black sesame seeds, plus extra to garnish

1 tbsp white sesame seeds, plus extra to garnish

1 large avocado, peeled, pitted and diced into 1-cm/½-inch dice

1 head iceberg lettuce, or thick cucumber slices, slightly hollowed out, to serve

SERVES 6–8

Seasoned raw fish with flavours of ginger, soy, sesame and spring onions/scallions, topped with avocado make a perfect Japanese-inspired light bite. A little bit of extra chilli/chile keeps things sprightly. You can serve this sashimi mix in lettuce cups or on cucumber slices.

Trim any sinew or bloodlines off the fish. Cut the flesh into 1-cm/¾-inch dice.

Stir the sugar into the soy sauce until it dissolves. Mix with the sesame oil, ginger and chilli. Combine the soy dressing with the fish. Gently fold through the spring onions, sesame seeds and avocado.

Serve with lettuce leaves to wrap around or pile onto thick slices of cucumber. Garnish with sesame seeds if you like.

MIXED SASHIMI

This pretty sashimi with ginger soy dressing and micro herb garnish uses salmon and tuna. Ask your fishmonger for the very best, freshest fish he has to offer. If you prefer, you can sear the fish quickly in a smoking-hot frying pan/skillet.

250 g/9 oz. sushi-grade tuna fillet

250 g/9 oz. skinless salmon fillet, pin bones removed

5-cm/2-inch piece of mooli/daikon radish

4 red-skinned radishes, trimmed

4 spring onions/scallions, thinly sliced on a diagonal

1 tbsp pickled ginger

micro herbs, baby rocket/arugula, or fresh coriander/cilantro

GINGER SOY DRESSING

½ fresh red chilli/chile, deseeded and sliced

½–1 tsp wasabi paste

2 tbsp soy sauce

juice of ½ a lime

SERVES 4

Cut the fish into thin slices and arrange on a platter.

Peel and cut the mooli into fine matchsticks. Cut the radishes into fine matchsticks. Mix the mooli, radishes and spring onions together and add to the platter. Add the pickled ginger, too.

To make the ginger soy dressing, mix together the chopped chilli, wasabi paste, soy sauce and lime juice in a little bowl.

Garnish the sashimi with the micro herbs and serve immediately with the ginger soy dressing.

BUNS & DUMPLINGS

BARBECUE PORK STEAMED BUNS

The pillowy-soft bread bun surrounding sweet and sticky char siu-style pork is just a heavenly combination.

1 batch Bread Dough (see page 8)

FILLING

1 tbsp sunflower or vegetable oil

1 shallot, chopped

2 tbsp dry sherry

350 g/12 oz. pork loin, diced

1 tsp crushed/minced garlic

2 tbsp clear honey

2 tbsp hoisin sauce

1 tsp Chinese five-spice powder

1 tbsp light soy sauce

steamer

16 squares of parchment paper

MAKES 16

To make the filling, heat the oil in a pan over a medium heat and add the shallot. Cook over a medium heat until softened and lightly caramelized, about 5–7 minutes. Pour in the sherry and cook for a few minutes. Lower the heat a little and add the pork. Cook, stirring, for a further 2 minutes or until lightly browned.

Meanwhile, in a separate bowl, mix the remaining ingredients with 2 tablespoons water. Add this to the pork mixture, stir well, cover and cook over a low heat for 1 hour, or until the sauce has thickened and the pork is tender. Check during cooking to ensure the sauce does not dry out. Add extra water if needed. Allow the pork mixture to cool and finely chop the meat.

Divide the dough into 16 portions and roll out each dough ball to 7.5 cm/3 inches in diameter (try to make the centre slightly thicker than the edges so that it can hold the filling). Cover each dough circle with a damp cloth to stop it from drying out.

Place a heaped tablespoon of the pork filling in the centre of each dough circle. Gather the edges to form pleats and pinch to seal the top of the bun. Working in batches if needed, place a bun on each square of parchment, then place in the steamer basket at least 5 cm/2 inches apart. Cover with oiled cling film/plastic wrap and let rise for 30 minutes.

Steam over boiling water for 8–10 minutes until the dough is light and fluffy. Let cool slightly, then serve.

SZECHUAN CHICKEN STEAMED BUNS

Traditionally filled with pork or bean paste, these fluffy buns are a popular and comforting dim sum option.

1 batch Fluffy Bread Dough (see page 8)

FILLING
4 chicken thighs

3 tbsp dark soy sauce

2 tbsp clear honey

1 tbsp Shaoxing (Chinese rice wine) or dry sherry

1–2 tbsp hot chilli/chili sauce

2–3 garlic cloves, crushed/minced

1 tbsp Szechuan peppercorns, crushed

steamer

MAKES 24

Put the chicken in a baking dish. Put the soy sauce in a bowl, mix in the honey, Shaoxing, chilli sauce, garlic and peppercorns, add to the chicken and turn to coat. Cover with foil or a lid and place in the fridge to marinate for 30 minutes–2 hours.

Preheat the oven to 180°C (350°F) Gas 4.

Transfer the baking dish, still covered, to the preheated oven and roast for 20 minutes, then uncover and cook a further 20 minutes until cooked through. Let cool, then remove the meat from the bones, shred it finely and mix the shredded meat with any marinade and juices left in the dish.

Divide the dough into 24 pieces and cover with a damp cloth. Take each piece of dough and, using your fingers, shape into a 6-cm/2½-inch disc. Put a teaspoon of the chicken filling in the centre of each one and gather up the dough around it. Pinch the edges together and twist to seal.

Place the buns, sealed edges up, on a sheet of parchment that will fit in your steamer, then place them into the steamer basket at least 2.5 cm/1 inches apart. You may have to do this in batches depending on the size of the steamer.

Steam over boiling water for 15–20 minutes until the buns are light and fluffy. Allow to cool slightly, then serve.

FRIED PRAWN & SCALLOP BUNS

These buns are intensely delicious, yet classy comfort food. With the surprise of a whole scallop in the centre, they are sure to be a winner.

2 spring onions/scallions, chopped

¼ head cabbage, chopped

400 g/14 oz. raw prawns/shrimp, peeled and deveined

3 tbsp oyster sauce

2 tbsp gochugaru (Korean chilli/chile flakes)

1 tbsp sesame oil

2 tbsp Shaoxing (Chinese rice wine) or dry sherry

1 batch Bread Dough (see page 8)

16 scallops

steamer

16 squares of parchment paper

MAKES 16

To make the filling, mix the spring onions and cabbage together in a large bowl. Mince the prawns by chopping them very finely with a sharp knife. Add these to the vegetables, along with the oyster sauce, chilli flakes, sesame oil and Shaoxing or sherry. Mix together well and chill in the fridge.

Divide the bread dough into 16 portions and roll out each dough ball to 7.5 cm/3 inches in diameter (try to make the centre slightly thicker than the edges so that it can hold the filling). Cover each dough circle with a damp cloth as you finish to stop it from drying out.

Place a tablespoon of the prawn filling in the centre of each dough circle and place a scallop on top. Gather the edges to form pleats and pinch to seal the top of the bun.

Place a bun on each square of parchment and then place into the steamer basket at least 5 cm/2 inches apart. You may have to do this in batches depending on the size of your steamer. Cover with oiled cling film/plastic wrap and allow to rise for 30 minutes.

Steam over boiling water for 8–10 minutes until the dough is light and fluffy. Let cool slightly, then serve.

CHICKEN TERIYAKI BAO

1 batch Bread Dough (see page 8)

CHICKEN TERIYAKI

5 chicken breasts or boneless chicken thighs

1 tbsp dark soy sauce

1 tbsp mirin (Japanese rice wine)

1 tbsp cooking sake (Chinese cooking rice wine)

2 tbsp soy sauce

2 tbsp clear honey

3 garlic cloves, chopped

salt and black pepper

TO SERVE

10 Little Gem/Bibb lettuce leaves

20 tomato slices

shredded spring onions/scallions

steamer

MAKES 10

This chicken teriyaki is best when it's left to marinate in the fridge for 48 hours, so start this recipe 2 days before you plan to cook it.

Slice the chicken breasts or thighs across the grain into 10 slices in total, then place into a casserole with all the other chicken teriyaki ingredients, 1 teaspoon salt, 1 tablespoon black pepper and 125 ml/½ cup water. Mix well, cover and place in the fridge to marinate for 48 hours.

When ready to cook, preheat the oven to 190°C (375°F) Gas 5.

Remove the lid from the chicken and roast in the oven for 20 minutes until cooked through (reduce the oven temperature slightly if the chicken is browning too much). Allow to cool.

Cut some parchment paper into 10 rectangles, 7 x 4 cm/2¾ x 1½ inches in size. Divide the dough into 10 portions. Roll out each one into an oval shape 1 cm/½ inch thick, then fold in half, placing a parchment rectangle in-between the folded dough.

Cut another 10 squares of parchment paper just larger than the buns. Working in batches if needed, place a bun on each square, on its side, then place in the steamer basket at least 5 cm/2 inches apart. Cover with oiled cling film/plastic wrap and leave to rise for 15 minutes. Steam over boiling water for 10 minutes until the buns are light and fluffy. Allow to cool before serving.

To serve, place lettuce and tomato in each bun, then add a piece of chicken and some shredded spring onions.

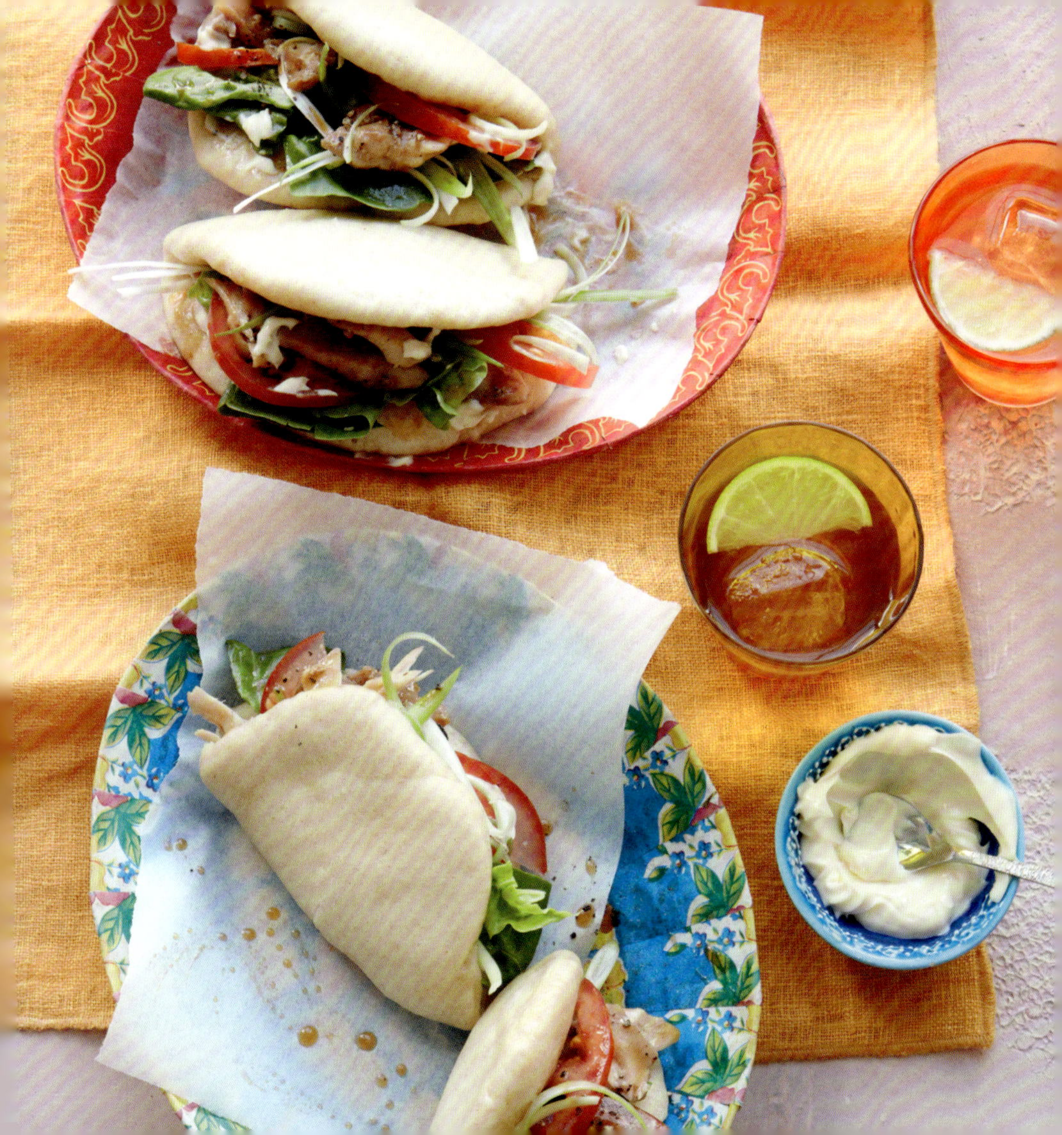

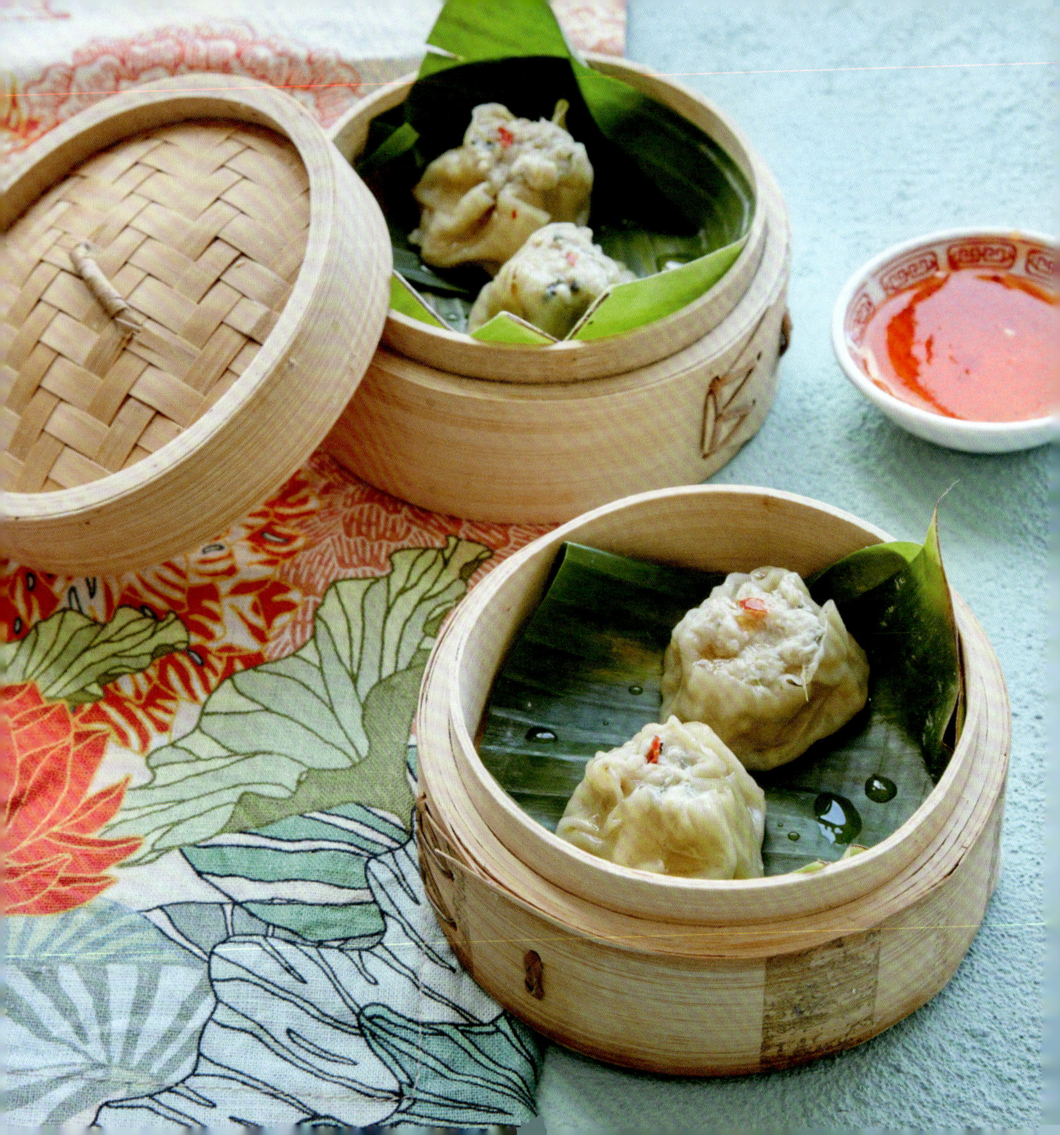

DUMPLINGS WITH MAKRUT LIME & LEMONGRASS

South-east Asian flavours take centre stage in these pretty dumplings.

- 2 garlic cloves, crushed/minced
- 4-cm/1½-inch piece fresh galangal or ginger, peeled and chopped
- 2 stalks lemongrass, finely chopped
- 8 makrut lime leaves, finely chopped
- 2 hot Thai chillies/chiles, deseeded and finely chopped
- 12 shallots, finely chopped
- 4 tbsp fish sauce or light soy sauce
- 500 g/1 lb. 2 oz. skinless, boneless chicken breast, minced/ground
- 4 tbsp coconut cream
- 50 small fresh wonton wrappers (2 packs)
- banana leaves, for steaming (optional)
- sweet chilli/chili sauce, to serve

steamer

MAKES 50

Using a small food processor or large mortar and pestle, grind the garlic, galangal or ginger, lemongrass, makrut lime leaves, chillies and shallots to form a paste – add a little of the fish sauce or soy sauce if needed. Transfer to a bowl, add the remaining fish or soy sauce, minced chicken and coconut cream and stir well.

Cut the wonton wrappers into rounds and discard the trimmings – keep them covered with a kitchen cloth so they don't dry out. Line the bamboo steamer with banana leaves (or parchment paper).

Put a wrapper on a dry surface and spread with a teaspoon of filling. Gather up the edges to form a basket shape, leaving the middle exposed. Drop it gently onto the work surface to flatten the bottom and settle the filling. Place in the steamer. Repeat until all are made, keeping the wrappers and the dumplings covered as you go and leaving space between the dumplings (cook in batches, if necessary).

Steam over boiling water for 8 minutes and serve immediately with sweet chilli sauce for dipping.

CHINESE POTSTICKERS

Potstickers are a form of Chinese dumpling that is fried, steamed, then fried again so they are both soft and crispy at the same time.

125 g/2 cups finely chopped Chinese cabbage

1 tsp salt

1 leek, trimmed and finely chopped

2 garlic cloves, crushed/minced

2 tbsp chopped fresh coriander/cilantro

250 g/1 cup minced/ground pork

24 gyoza wrappers

2 tbsp vegetable oil

your favourite dipping sauce, to serve

baking sheet lined with baking parchment

SERVES 4

Put the cabbage in a large mixing bowl with the salt and toss well to coat. Transfer to a colander and leave to drain for 1 hour to remove as much water as possible from the cabbage. Squeeze out any remaining water and put the cabbage in a clean large mixing bowl with the leek, garlic and coriander. Gradually work in the pork until combined.

Working one at a time, lay the gyoza wrappers out flat and place a teaspoon of the mixture on one half of each wrapper. Dampen the edges with a little cold water, fold the wrapper over the filling and carefully press the edges together to seal.

Preheat the oven to 110°C (225°F) Gas ¼ (or the lowest setting).

Heat 1 tablespoon of the oil in a wok or large non-stick frying pan/skillet set over a high heat. Add half the dumplings and fry for about 1 minute until the bottoms are golden. Add 100 ml/⅓ cup water and simmer, partially covered, for 5 minutes, until the water has evaporated. Cook for a further 2–3 minutes until the bottoms are crispy. Transfer the dumplings to the prepared baking sheet, turn off the oven and set in the still-warm oven while you cook the remaining dumplings in the same way.

Serve the dumplings with your favourite dipping sauce.

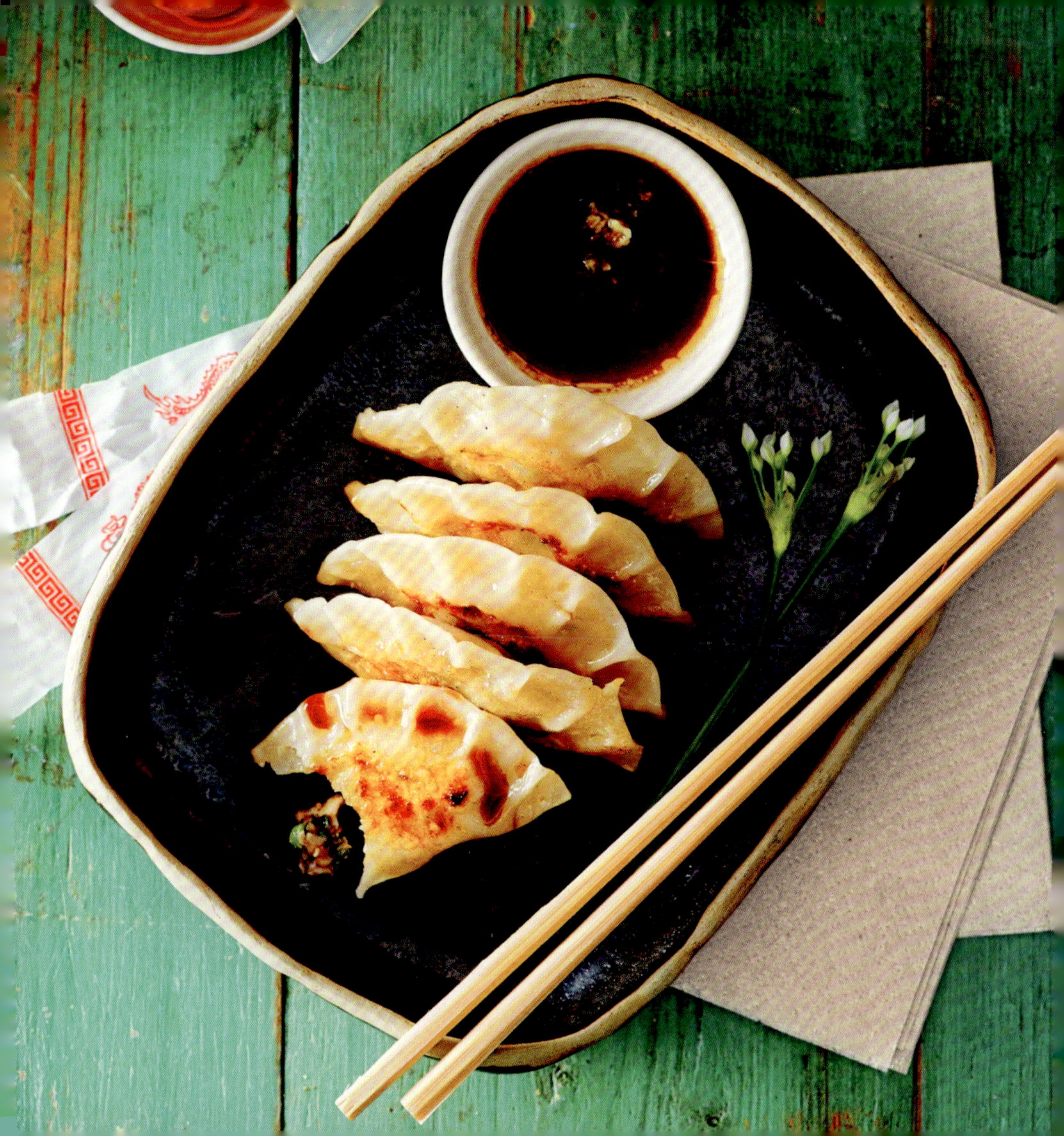

TRADITIONAL PRAWN DUMPLINGS

Also known as *har gao*, these little dumplings are one of the most iconic dim sum dishes.

50 g/1¾ oz. firm tofu, drained and minced

150 g/5½ oz. uncooked prawns/shrimp, shelled and deveined

1 tsp fresh ginger, peeled and grated

1 tsp crushed/minced garlic

½ tsp Shaoxing rice wine

½ tsp salt

½ tsp caster/granulated sugar

½ tsp ground white pepper

1 tsp olive oil

1 tsp cornflour/cornstarch

CRYSTAL SKIN DOUGH

100 g/¾ cup wheat starch

50 g/½ cup tapioca starch

a pinch of salt

150 ml/⅔ cup boiling (not hot) water

DIPPING SAUCE

1 small piece fresh ginger, peeled and grated

6 tbsp black vinegar

a bamboo steamer lined with parchment paper

MAKES 16

Squeeze out the excess water from the tofu and finely mince using a sharp knife.

Chop each prawn into 4–5 small pieces and place in a bowl.

Add the drained and minced tofu, ginger, garlic, Shaoxing rice wine, salt, sugar, white pepper, oil and cornflour. Mix well and set aside in the fridge to marinate while you make the dough.

For the dough, in a large mixing bowl, combine the wheat starch, tapioca starch and salt. Add the boiling water and mix with a wooden spoon until a dough is formed.

Transfer to a lightly floured surface and knead until smooth. Separate the dough in half and roll into two equal cylinders, about 2.5 cm/1 inch diameter. Wrap in cling film/plastic wrap and rest until needed.

Divide the dough into 16 equal balls. On a lightly floured surface use a rolling pin to flatten the dough balls into thin discs, about 5 cm/2 inch diameter. Cover the finished skins with a damp kitchen cloth as you work so that they don't dry out.

Place a large teaspoon of filling neatly into the centre of a skin. Fold the skin in half over the filling. Pinch one end together and start to crimp the edge by making small folds to form pleats to create the traditional crescent shape.

Put the dumplings into the prepared steamer. Steam over boiling water for 15–20 minutes or until the skin is transparent and the prawns are pink.

To make the dipping sauce, stir the minced ginger into the black vinegar. Serve the dumplings hot alongside the dipping sauce.

BUNS & DUMPLINGS **41**

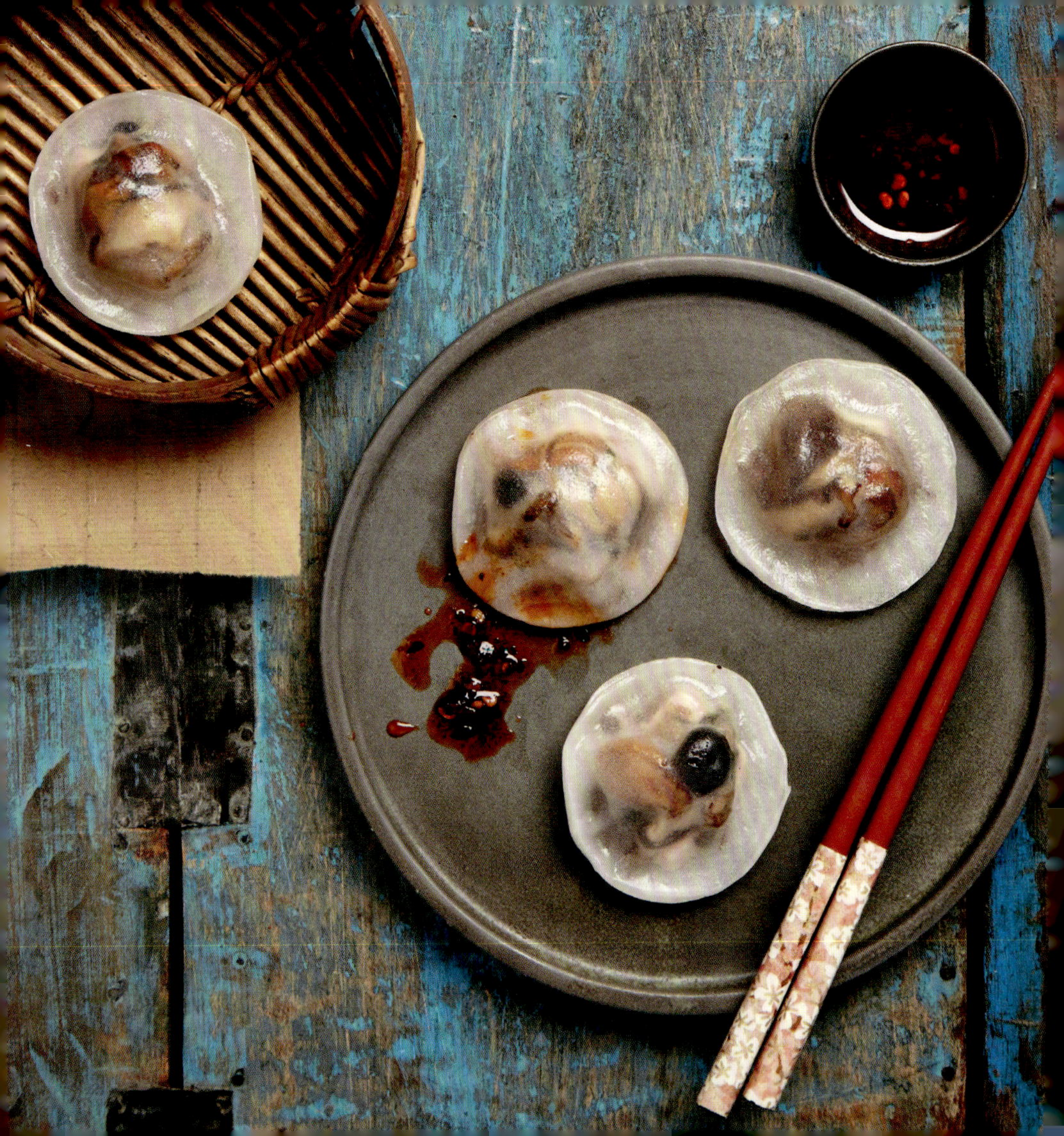

SALMON & MUSHROOM DUMPLINGS

Salmon works well with the light texture of a crystal skin dough, with the pretty pink colour contrasting against the white in these tasty bites.

1 batch of Crystal Skin Dough (see page 40)

1 oyster mushroom

1 bunch enoki mushrooms

3 shiitaki mushrooms

20 g/¼ cup chanterelle mushrooms

1 tbsp sunflower oil

1 garlic clove, finely chopped

1 small salmon fillet

1 tbsp grated fresh ginger

1 bunch of Chinese chive stalks, white parts removed

chilli/chile oil, to serve

small round pastry cutter

bamboo steamer, lined with non-stick baking parchment

MAKES 12

Prepare the crystal skin dough following the recipe on page 40, and make the filling while the dough is resting.

Slice the mushrooms into small, even pieces. Heat the sunflower oil in a frying pan/skillet and fry the mushrooms and garlic over a medium heat until fragrant. Set aside to cool, discarding any excess juice.

Roll out the crystal skin dough and stamp out 24 circles using the small round pastry cutter. Portion the salmon fillet into 12 pieces and cut the Chinese chive stalks into 3-cm/2-inch lengths.

Place a salmon piece in the centre of a skin, add a sprinkle of grated ginger and a chive piece neatly on the top. Lastly, top with a teaspoon of the cooked mushrooms. Cover with another round skin and press around the edge to seal.

Place the dumplings into the lined bamboo steamer and steam over boiling water until transparent and the salmon is cooked through. Serve hot with chilli oil for dipping.

KIMCHI NOODLE DUMPLINGS

Traditionally kimchi is quite fiery, so you can adjust the amount of chilli/hot red pepper flakes to your personal heat preferences. Add more if you dare!

150 g/⅔ cup minced/ground pork

150 g/scant 1 cup cooked prawns/shrimp, peeled and very finely chopped

100 g/4 oz. kimchi

2 tsp dark soy sauce

½ beaten egg

20 gyoza wrappers

4 tbsp vegetable oil

TO SERVE

your favourite dipping sauce

spring onions/scallions, thinly sliced

a baking sheet lined with baking parchment

SERVES 4

Put the pork, prawns, kimchi, soy sauce and beaten egg in a large bowl and mix together until evenly combined.

Working one at a time, lay the gyoza wrappers out flat and place a teaspoon of the mixture on one half of each wrapper. Dampen the edges with a little cold water, fold the wrapper over the filling and carefully press the edges together to seal.

Preheat the oven to 110°C (225°F) Gas ¼ (or the lowest heat setting).

Heat the oil in a wok or large non-stick frying pan/skillet set over a high heat. Add half the dumplings and fry for about 1 minute until the bottoms are golden. Add 125 ml/½ cup water to the pan, cover and simmer for 5 minutes until the filling is heated through. Remove the lid and cook for a further 1–2 minutes until the bottoms are crispy. Transfer the dumplings to the prepared baking sheet, turn off the oven and set in the still-warm oven while you cook the remaining dumplings in the same way.

Arrange the dumplings on warmed plates and serve with dipping sauce, scattered with spring onions.

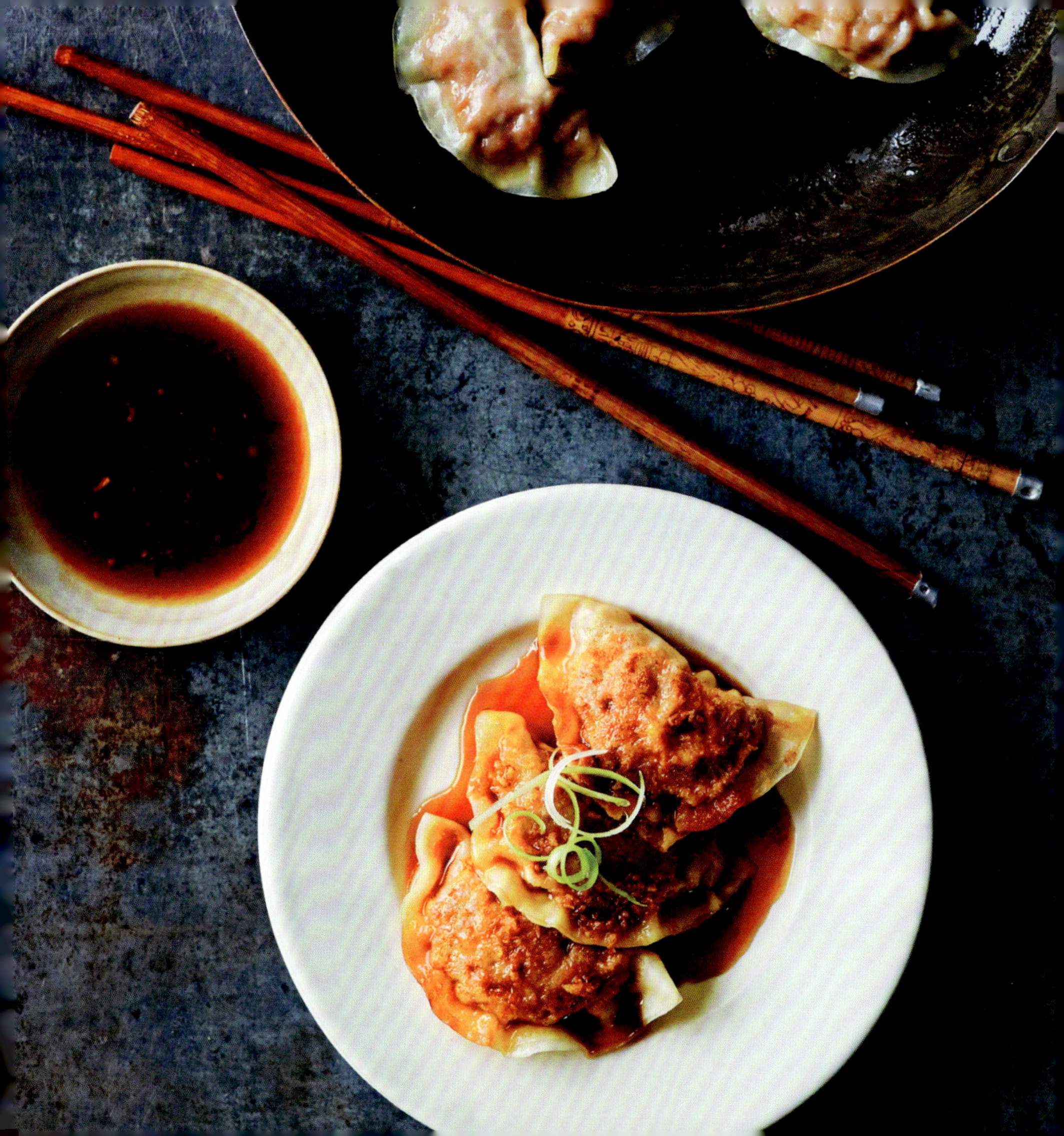

WONTON PORK MONEYBAGS

These can be cooked and served straight from bamboo steamers. If you cook three tiers at a time, you can serve the first batch while the next one is cooking. The bacon isn't a traditional Chinese ingredient, but it means you need less salt.

500 g/1 lb. 2 oz. minced/ground pork

125 g/1 cup raw prawns/shrimp, peeled and deveined

3 slices smoked streaky/fatty bacon, chopped

1 tsp crushed pepper, preferably Szechuan

1 egg white

2 tsp sesame oil

3-cm/1½-inch piece fresh ginger, peeled and grated

1 garlic clove, crushed/minced

2 tsp cornflour/cornstarch

4 spring onions/scallions

4 canned water chestnuts, finely diced

1 Chinese snake/yard-long bean or 4 green/French beans, thinly sliced

50 small fresh wonton wrappers (2 packs)

salt

banana leaves, for steaming (optional)

soy sauce, to serve

MAKES 50

Put the pork, prawns and bacon into a food processor and blend to a purée. With the motor running, add the pepper, egg white, sesame oil, ginger, garlic, cornflour and 2 teaspoons salt.

Finely chop the spring onions crossways, transfer to a mixing bowl, then add the pork mixture, water chestnuts and bean(s). Mix well – using your hands is the best way.

Cut the wonton wrappers into rounds and discard the trimmings – keep them covered with a damp kitchen cloth so they don't dry out. Line the steamer basket with banana leaves (or parchment paper).

Put a tablespoon of the pork filling in the centre of each round wrapper. Use a teaspoon to smooth the mixture almost to the edges.

Cup the wonton in the palm of your hand. Gather up your hand, pushing down with the teaspoon: you will achieve an open-topped, pleated, money-bag-shaped container filled with mixture. Drop it gently onto the work surface to flatten the bottom and settle the filling. Place in the steamer. Repeat until all are made, keeping the wrappers and the dumplings covered as you go and leaving space between the dumplings (cook in batches, if necessary).

Steam over boiling water for about 7–10 minutes, or until cooked through. Serve hot with a simple soy sauce dip.

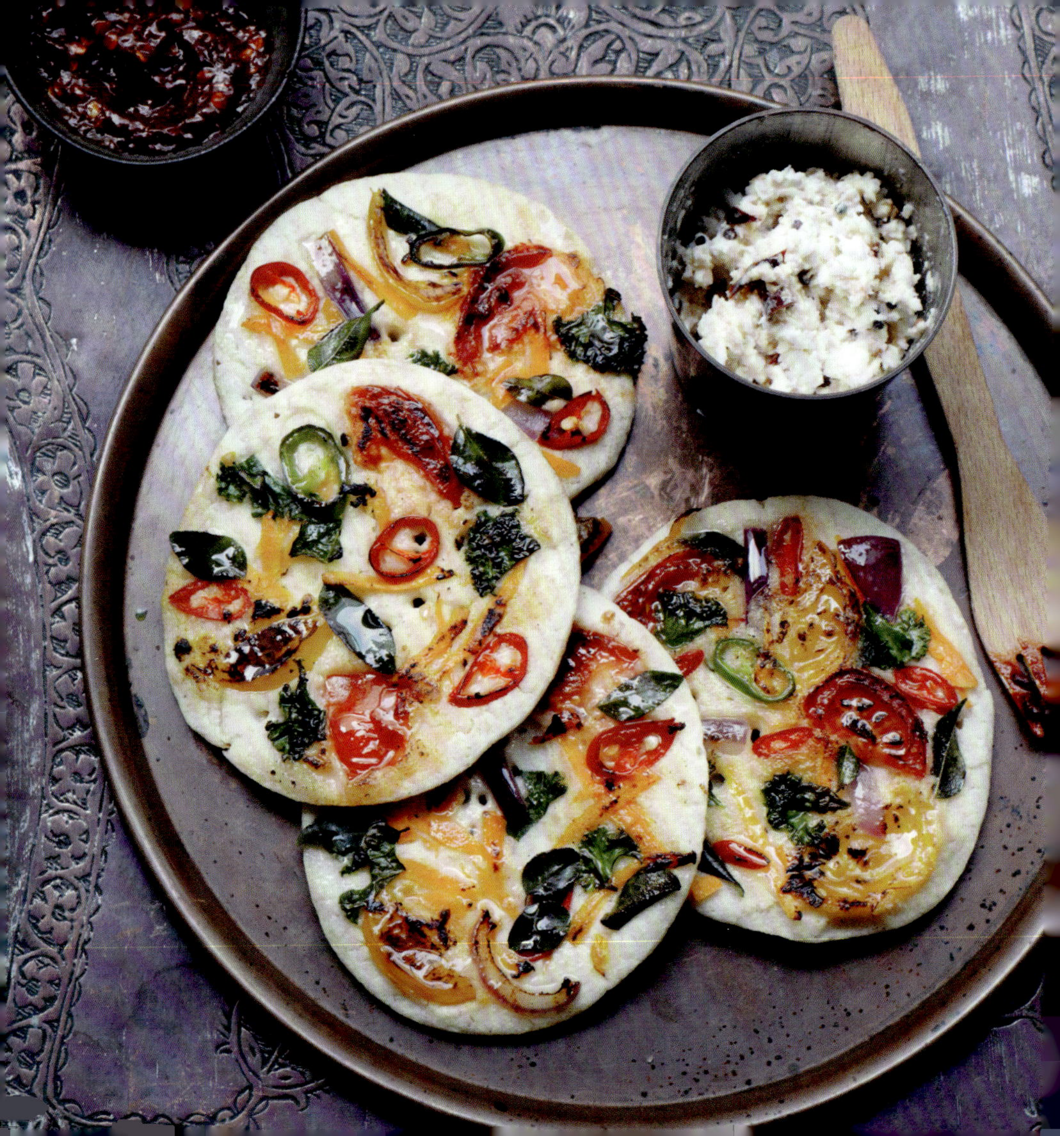

ROLLS & PANCAKES

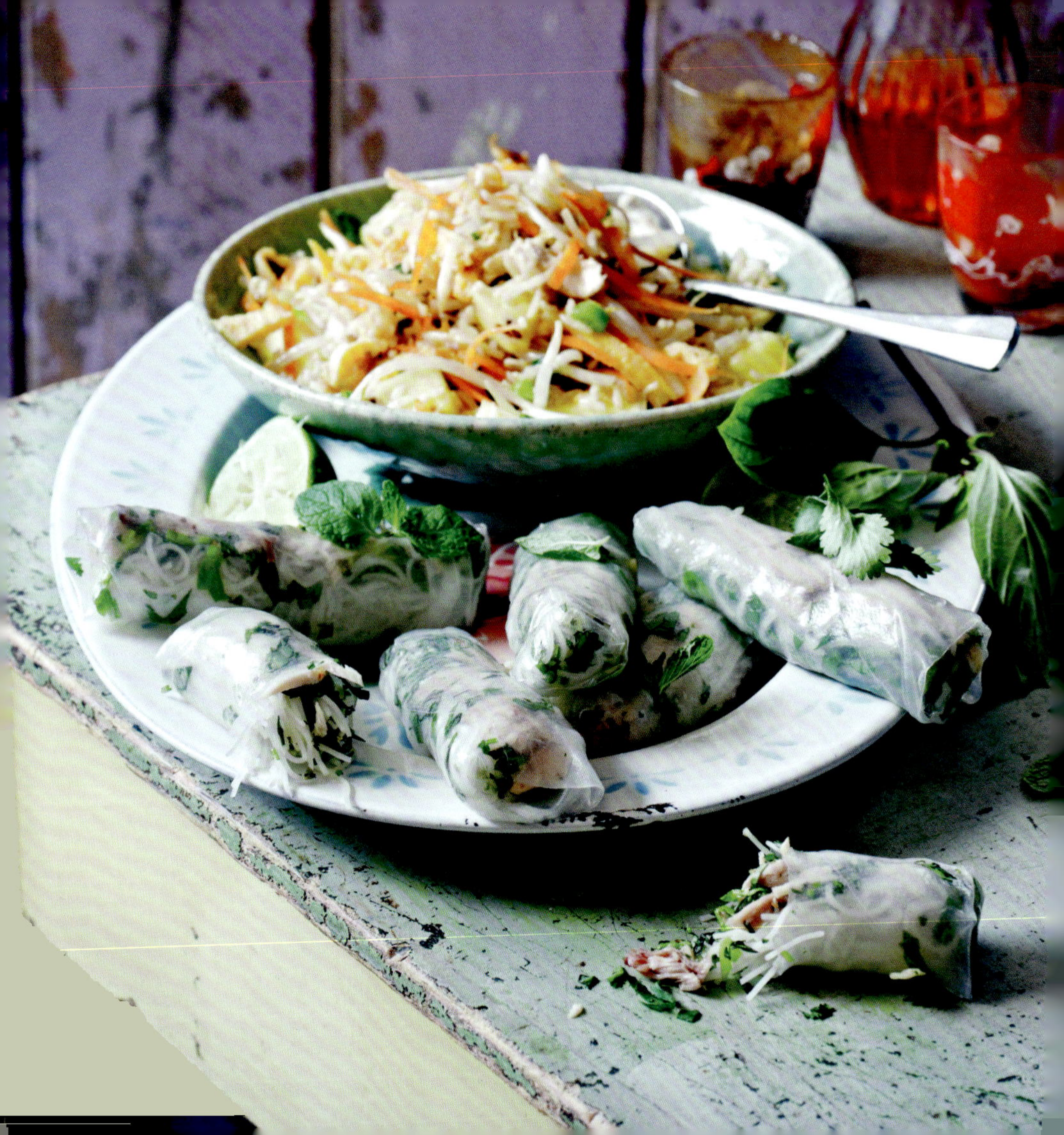

SUMMER ROLLS

These refreshing, fragrant rolls are the perfect addition to any sunny meal and go particularly well with a fresh Asian slaw.

60 g/2 oz. rice vermicelli

8 rice paper wrappers (22-cm/8½-inch diameter)

3 tbsp chopped fresh mint

3 tbsp chopped fresh coriander/cilantro

2 lettuce leaves, chopped

1½ tbsp fish sauce

2 tbsp lime juice

2 garlic cloves, crushed/minced

1½ tbsp caster/granulated sugar

½ tsp sweet chilli sauce

2 tbsp hoisin sauce

1 tsp finely chopped peanuts

MAKES 8

Bring a medium saucepan of water to boil. Boil the rice vermicelli for 3–5 minutes, or until al dente, and drain.

Fill a large bowl with warm water. Dip one rice wrapper into the water for 1 second to soften. Lay the wrapper flat. In a row across the centre, place a handful of vermicelli, mint, coriander and lettuce, leaving about 5 cm/2 inches uncovered on each side. Fold the uncovered sides inward, then tightly roll the wrapper, beginning at the end with the lettuce. Repeat with remaining ingredients.

In a small bowl, mix the fish sauce, 4 tablespoons water, lime juice, garlic, sugar and chilli sauce. In another small bowl, mix the hoisin sauce and peanuts.

Serve immediately with the summer rolls for dipping.

VEGAN TEMAKI ROLLS WITH SEED PÂTÉ

This hand-rolled sushi is really easy to make. Temakis are a great choice for parties since they are best rolled directly at the table, just before eating, and everybody can join in. Prepare and serve all ingredients in the middle of the table and let the fun begin!

FERMENTED SEED PÂTÉ

240 g/2 cups pumpkin seeds

50 ml/scant ¼ cup olive oil

1 garlic clove

¼ tsp turmeric powder

1 tbsp nutritional yeast (optional)

3 tsp vegan rice or barley miso

2 tsp lemon juice

¼ tsp salt

black pepper

MAKES 250 G/2½ CUPS

TEMAKI ROLLS

2 medium carrots

1 ripe avocado

2 handfuls rocket/arugula or 50 g/1 cup alfalfa sprouts, plus extra to serve

3 spring onions/scallions

6 sheets of nori seaweed

2 cups sauerkraut or other fermented vegetables, plus extra to serve

soy sauce, to serve

MAKES 12

First make the pâté. Soak the pumpkin seeds in 840 ml/ 3½ cups water for 2–3 days, until slightly fermented, without changing the soaking water.

Discard the soaking water and rinse the seeds thoroughly under running water. Drain well. Place in a high-speed blender, together with the remaining ingredients and 60 ml/¼ cup water. Blend until smooth, using a tamper tool to push down the ingredients. If you don't own a high-speed blender, the pâté will probably turn out chunkier in a less powerful blender, and more water will need to be added, resulting in a somewhat runnier consistency. Let sit in the fridge for another day; the flavours really develop in this final stage of setting. There will be some leftovers, but you can store these in the fridge and use within a week.

Wash and julienne the carrots. Peel the avocado, slice in half, discard the stone and cut both halves in strips. Wash the rocket or sprouts and pat dry. Take only the green parts of the spring onions, wash them well and cut into 10-cm/4-inch pieces. Cut each nori sheet in half with scissors.

Make sure your hands are dry before starting. Place a piece of nori (shiny side down) in the palm of your hand and add 1½ tablespoons of pumpkin seed pâté. Spread it gently on the left third of the nori sheet. Place your chosen fillings diagonally over the pate. Do not overfill; a couple of carrot matchsticks, 1 slice of avocado, 1 tablespoon of sauerkraut and some greens are more than enough.

Fold the bottom left corner of the nori over and begin rolling into a cone shape. Wet the edge with little water and seal. Continue until all nori is used.

Serve the temaki rolls with more fermented vegetables, condiments, some soy sauce and leftover greens.

ROLLS & PANCAKES

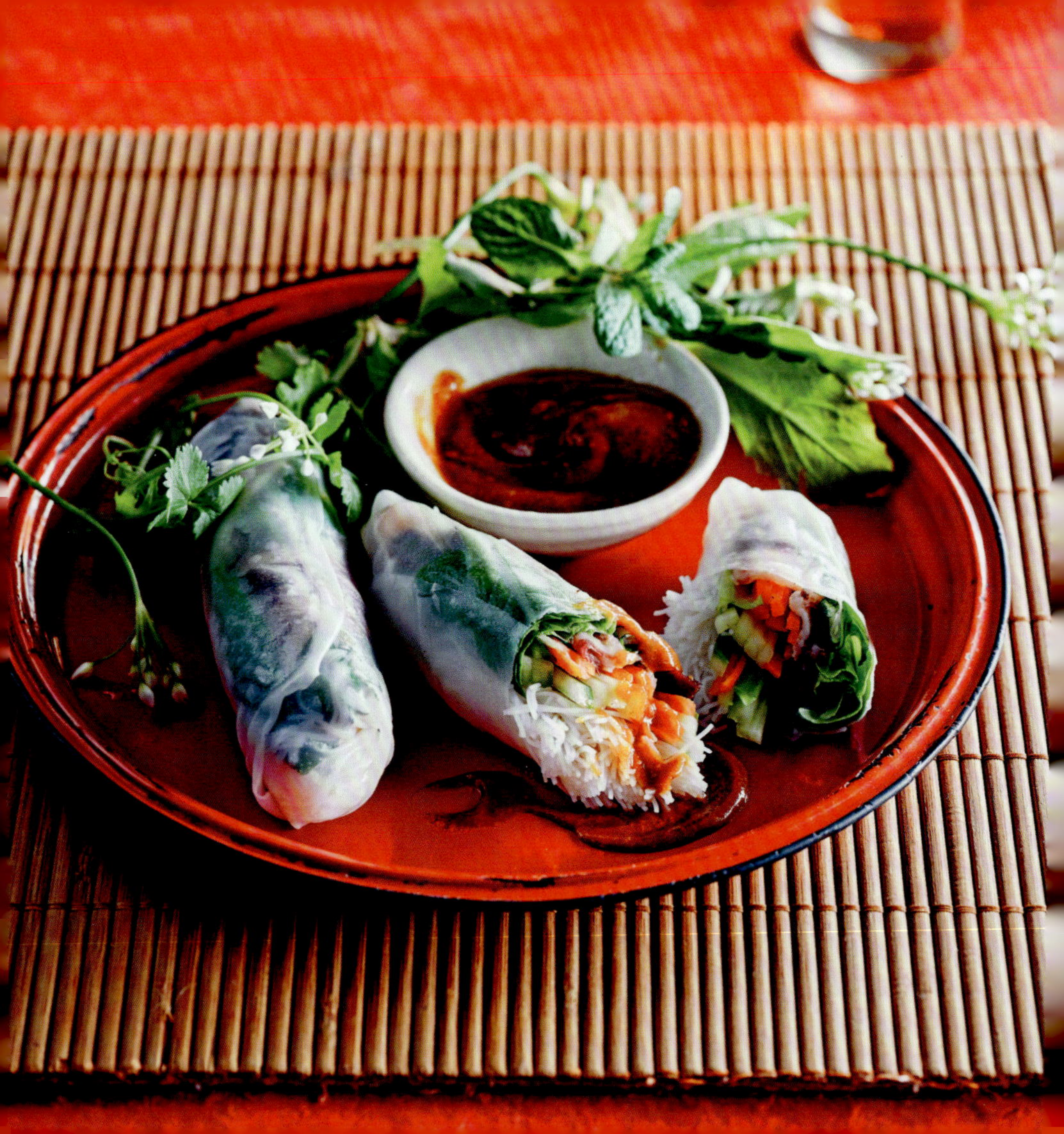

SMOKED DUCK RICE PAPER ROLLS

100 g/3½ oz. rice vermicelli noodles

2 tsp fish sauce

2 tsp lime juice

2 tsp caster/granulated sugar

8 x 20-cm/8-inch dried rice paper wrappers

100 g/3½ oz. smoked duck breast (or use smoked salmon or smoked trout)

100 g/3 cups thinly sliced lettuce

1 carrot, peeled and cut into thin batons

½ cucumber, deseeded and cut into batons

20 fresh Thai basil leaves

HOISIN & PEANUT DIPPING SAUCE

2 tbsp hoisin sauce

1 tbsp smooth peanut butter

1 tbsp warm water

2 tsp lime juice

1 tsp dark soy sauce

¼ tsp caster/granulated sugar

SERVES 4

Vietnamese summer rolls are named due to their refreshing nature and are typically served in summer months with many different fillings.

Put the noodles in a bowl, cover with boiling water and soak for 30 minutes until softened. Drain the noodles, pat dry and transfer to a large mixing bowl. Whisk the fish sauce, lime juice and sugar together until the sugar is dissolved and pour it over the noodles. Toss well and set aside.

Put all the ingredients for the dipping sauce in a small saucepan set over a low heat. Heat gently, stirring until the peanut butter is softened and the sauce smooth. Remove from the heat and set aside to cool.

Working one at a time, dip the rice paper wrappers into a bowl of warm water for about a minute until softened and then pat dry on paper towels.

Lay each wrapper out flat and top with a few noodles, the smoked duck slices, shredded lettuce, carrot, cucumber and basil leaves. Fold the ends of the rice paper over the filling and then roll up tightly to form parcels. Serve with the dipping sauce.

EGG ROLLS

There is something so satisfying about a Chinese egg roll. Maybe it's the crunch; maybe it's the texture; maybe it's something about how pork and cabbage come together so well when hugged between egg roll wrappers and deep fried. Whatever it is, they're delicious!

3 tbsp olive oil

1 tsp salt

1 tsp black pepper

1 tsp ground ginger

1 tsp garlic powder

450 g/1 lb. pork shoulder

1 litre/quart groundnut/peanut oil, for frying

2 tbsp plain/all-purpose flour

120 g/2 cups cabbage, shredded

1 carrot, grated/shredded

8 x 18-cm/7-inch square egg roll wrappers

2 tbsp sesame seeds (optional)

SWEET & SOUR SAUCE

1 tbsp soy sauce

3½ tbsp caster/granulated sugar

3½ tbsp white vinegar

zest of 1 unwaxed orange

meat thermometer

MAKES 8

Preheat the oven to 180°C (350°F) Gas 4.

Spread the oil, salt, ground black pepper, ginger and garlic powder on the pork shoulder.

Set the meat on a rack set into a roasting pan. Roast for about 20 minutes, and then reduce the heat to 160°C (325°F) Gas 3. Continue to cook for 1–2 hours until an instant-read thermometer inserted into the shoulder reads 85°C (185°F). Remove the pork from the oven and let stand for about 30 minutes until cool enough to handle. Shred the pork.

Mix the flour with 2 tablespoons water in a bowl into a paste.

ROLLS & PANCAKES

In a separate bowl combine the cabbage, carrots and shredded pork and mix them together.

Lay out one egg roll wrapper with a corner pointed toward you. Place about 20 g/¼ cup of the cabbage, carrot and shredded pork mixture onto the wrapper and fold the corner up over the mixture. Fold the left and right corners toward the centre and continue to roll. Brush a bit of the flour paste on the final corner to help seal.

In a large frying pan/skillet, heat the oil to about 190°C (375°F).

Place the egg rolls into the heated oil and fry, turning occasionally, until golden brown. Remove from the oil and drain on paper towels or a wire rack.

Put on a serving plate and top with sesame seeds if desired.

To make the sweet and sour sauce, mix all the ingredients together in a mixing bowl with 1 tablespoon water. Transfer to a small saucepan and bring to the boil, then remove from the heat. Pour the sauce into a small bowl and serve with the egg rolls.

ROLLS & PANCAKES

VEGETARIAN SPRING ROLLS

These crispy spring rolls are usually a staple order on any Chinese takeaway. The filling can be varied to suit personal tastes. This recipe uses a vegetarian filling, but you could also add minced/ground chicken or pork as a variation.

15 g/⅔ cup dried black cloud ear fungus

25 g/1 oz. cellophane noodles (

75 g/3 oz. carrots

50 g/a small handful of mangetout/snow peas

1 tbsp vegetable oil

1 tsp freshly grated ginger

25 g/scant ½ cup spinach, torn

1 tbsp light or dark soy sauce

1 tbsp oyster sauce

a pinch of black pepper

16 large spring roll wrappers

1–2 eggs, lightly beaten

sweet chilli sauce, to serve

a baking sheet lined with baking parchment

SERVES 4

Put the mushrooms in a large bowl, cover with boiling water and soak for 20 minutes until softened. Drain, pat dry with paper towels and slice thinly, discarding any tough stalks. Set aside.

Meanwhile, put the noodles in a bowl, cover with boiling water and soak for 30 minutes until softened. Drain the noodles and pat dry with paper towels. Using scissors, cut the noodles into 5 cm/2 inch lengths and set aside.

Cut the carrots into 5-cm/2-inch batons and the mangetout into similar-sized shreds.

Heat the oil in a wok or large frying pan/skillet and stir-fry the ginger for a few seconds before adding the carrots and mangetout. Stir-fry for 2 minutes before adding the mushrooms, spinach, soy sauce, oyster sauce and black pepper. Stir well and remove the pan from the heat. Stir in the noodles and set aside to cool.

Working one wrapper at a time, trim each to 12 x 18 cm/4¾ x 7 inches, lay out flat and brush the top with beaten egg. Place a tablespoon of the cooled filling in a log shape along one edge of the wrapper. Roll over once, then fold the ends in and over the roll. Continue to roll up tightly to form a sealed parcel.

Preheat the oven to 110°C (225°F) Gas ¼, or the lowest heat setting.

Pour vegetable oil into a wok or large saucepan to reach about 5 cm/2 inches up the side and set over a medium–high heat. Heat until a cube of bread dropped into the oil crisps in 30 seconds. Deep-fry the rolls a few at a time for 1–2 minutes until crisp and golden. Drain on paper towels and transfer the rolls to the prepared baking sheet.

Turn off the oven and set in the still-warm oven while you cook the remaining rolls in the same way.

Serve the spring rolls hot with sweet chilli sauce.

ROLLS & PANCAKES

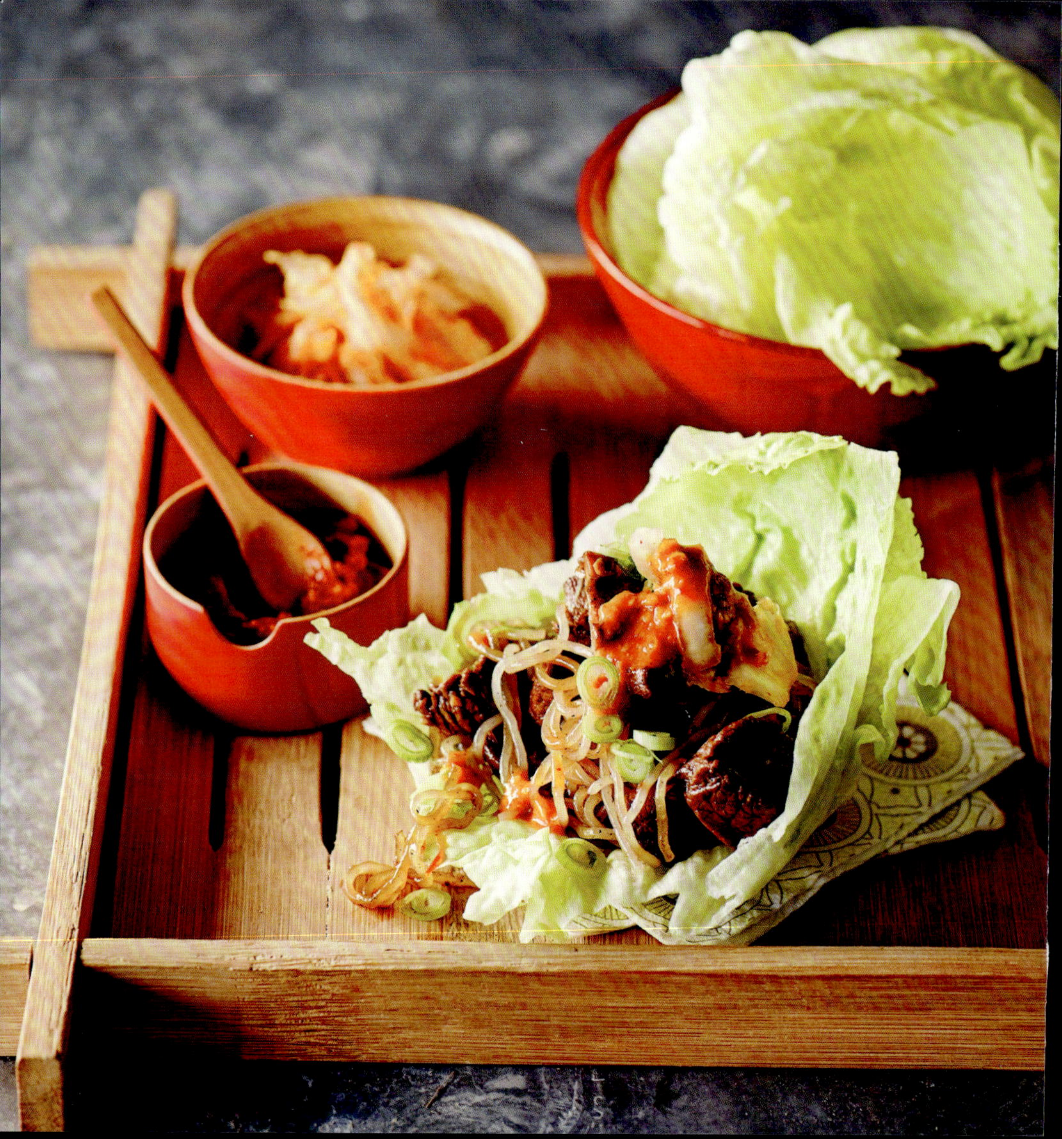

BEEF BULGOGI & RICE NOODLE WRAPS

500 g/1 lb. beef rib-eye steak

2 tbsp light or dark soy sauce

2 tbsp soft brown sugar

1 Asian shallot, finely chopped

1 garlic clove, crushed

2 tsp sesame oil, plus extra for dressing

½ tsp Chinese five-spice powder

125 g/4 oz. sweet potato noodles

2 tbsp peanut oil

125 g/4 oz. shiitake mushrooms, trimmed and cut into quarters

4 tbsp kimchi

Ssamjang sauce (see page 11)

SERVES 4

The Korean word *bulgogi* means 'fire meat' and refers to marinated and grilled beef, which is here stir-fried, wrapped in lettuce leaves and topped with kimchi and ssamjang.

Begin by preparing the beef. Thinly slice the steak and arrange in a single layer in a wide, shallow dish. Combine the soy sauce, sugar, shallot, garlic, sesame oil and Chinese five-spice powder, and pour over the beef. Set aside to marinate for at least 1 hour.

Plunge the sweet potato noodles into a pan of boiling water and cook for 4–5 minutes until al dente. Drain, refresh under cold water and drain again. Shake the noodles dry and dress with a little sesame oil to prevent them from sticking together. Set aside.

Heat the oil in a wok or large frying pan/skillet set over a medium heat until it starts to shimmer. Add the beef in batches and stir-fry for 2–3 minutes until golden. Remove with a slotted spoon. Add the mushrooms and any remaining marinade and stir-fry for 1 minute. Return the beef to the pan along with the noodles and stir-fry for 1 minute, until everything is heated through.

Divide the noodles between bowls and serve with lettuce leaves, kimchi and ssamjang sauce. Wrap, roll and eat.

PEKING-STYLE DUCK PANCAKE WRAPS

4 duck breasts, weighing about 150 g/5¼ oz. each

4 tbsp dark soy sauce

1 tbsp clear honey

2 tsp Chinese five-spice powder

1 tbsp groundnut/peanut oil

salt

TO SERVE

1 cucumber, cut into matchsticks

24 Chinese Peking duck pancakes

125 ml/½ cup hoisin sauce

6 spring onions/scallions, halved lengthways and crossways

sesame seeds

steamer

24 squares of parchment paper, 12-cm/5-inch square

MAKES 24

These wraps always go down well at parties and are perfect picnic fare. The paper wrappers keep them moist and stop them sticking together if you prepare them in advance. Chinese Peking duck pancakes can usually be found in Chinese grocers.

Score the duck fat diagonally at 5-mm/¼-inch intervals and rub in about 1 tablespoon salt.

Mix the soy sauce, honey and five-spice powder in a flat glass or ceramic dish. Put the duck breasts, skin-side up, in the marinade, moving them about so the flesh is coated. Cover and set aside in the fridge to marinate for at least 2 hours.

Remove the duck from the marinade and pat dry with paper towels.

Heat the oil in a frying pan/skillet over a medium heat, add the duck breasts, skin-side down, and cook for 8 minutes. Pour off the fat from the pan, then turn the breasts and cook the other side for 4 minutes. Remove from the pan and let cool.

Slice each duck breast diagonally into 12 strips.

Place the pancakes in the steamer basket lined with parchment paper and steam over boiling water for 5 minutes.

When filling, work on 3–4 pancakes at a time and keep the others covered with a damp kitchen cloth so they don't dry out. Spread a teaspoon of hoisin sauce on each pancake, then add a couple of pieces of duck, a few strips of cucumber, a piece of spring onion and some sesame seeds. Fold up the bottom, then the sides. Wrap the pieces of parchment paper around the pancakes in the same way, then cover with a cloth until ready to serve.

ROLLS & PANCAKES

JAPANESE OKONOMIYAKI PANCAKES

These chunky cabbage-based pancakes are a great snack to make with friends, frying them up one at a time and adding different toppings. Originally from Osaka, the name means 'grill as you like it', so you really can make it your own and adapt the ingredients to taste. Omit the prawns/shrimp for a vegetarian option.

100 g/¾ cup white spelt flour

¼ tsp baking powder

½ tsp sea salt

150 ml/⅔ cup instant dashi, or fish or vegetable stock

2 eggs

300 g/10 oz. cabbage, thinly sliced

3 spring onions/scallions, finely chopped diagonally, reserve some for garnish

2 tbsp vegetable oil

100 g/3½ oz. raw prawns/shrimp, peeled and deveined

2 tbsp kewpie (Japanese mayonnaise), or normal mayonnaise

2 tbsp Okonomiyaki sauce (see tip, right)

2 tbsp bonito flakes (dried, smoked tuna flakes)

1 tbsp pickled sushi ginger

frying pan/skillet with a fitted lid

MAKES 2

In a large bowl combine the flour, baking powder and salt. Whisk in the dashi (or fish or vegetable stock) and eggs. Add the cabbage and most of the spring onions and combine together.

In the non-stick frying pan/skillet add a tablespoon of the vegetable oil and heat over a medium-high heat. Add half the batter in a neat round shape about 15 cm/6 inches in diameter; don't flatten it out, as okonomiyaki should be thick.

Place half the prawns on top so they sit into the batter, cover the pan with the fitted lid and cook for about 3–4 minutes until the bottom is set and lightly golden.

Carefully turn over, place the lid back on and cook for a further 3–4 minutes until the prawns are cooked through and the surface is golden. Turn over one last time and cook for 2 minutes with the lid off.

Slide the pancake onto a plate, then drizzle over half of the kewpie or mayonnaise and the Okonomiyaki sauce, top with the bonito flakes and remaining spring onions.

Serve immediately with the pickled ginger on the side. Repeat to make the second pancake.

Tip: You can buy Okonomiyaki sauce (as well as kewpie mayonnaise, dashi stock and bonito flakes) in an Asian market, or online. Or you can make your own less sugary version of Okonomiyaki sauce at home by mixing 1 tablespoon soy sauce with 1 teaspoon rice vinegar. It will be too thin to drizzle on top, so serve it as a dipping sauce on the side.

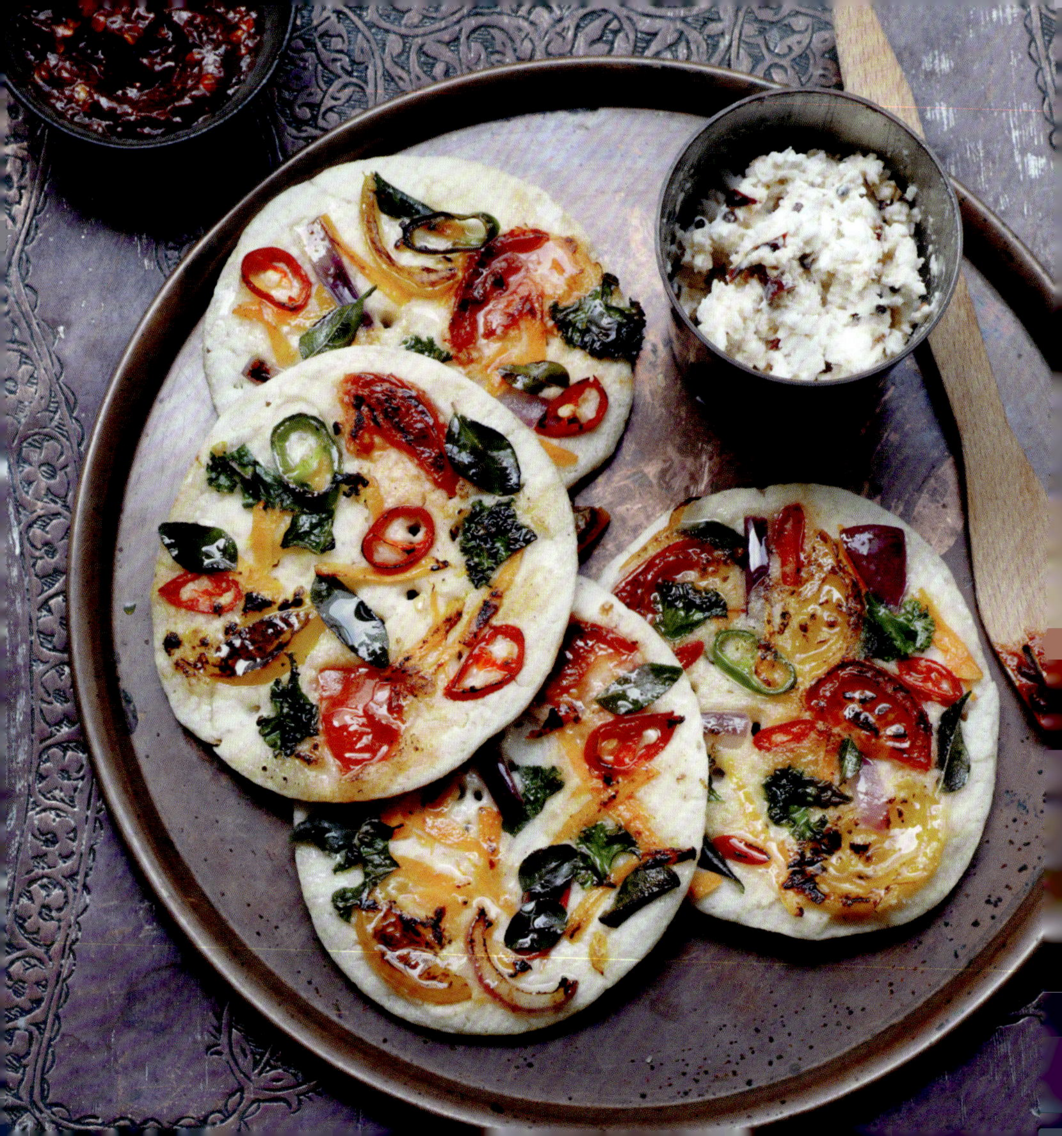

INDIAN VEGETABLE PANCAKES

vegetable oil, for frying

1–2 green chillies/chiles, to taste, thinly sliced

3 fresh or dried curry leaves, chopped

1 red onion, thinly sliced

2 tomatoes, finely chopped

1 carrot, grated

small handful of chopped kale

coconut chutney or spicy sambar chilli/chile paste, to serve

QUICK BATTER

300 g/2 cups coarse semolina flour

300 g/1⅓ cups plain or soy yogurt

1 tsp lemon juice

1 tsp bicarbonate of soda/baking soda

1 tsp salt

pinch of asafoetida powder

MAKES 10–14

These Indian thick semolina pancakes are also known as 'oothapam'. This is a quick version of the traditional fermented recipe, which doesn't come out as thick as the original, but is just as delicious and makes a perfect snack.

For the quick batter, mix all the ingredients together with enough water to make a thick pouring consistency. Set aside for 10–15 minutes.

Add ½ tablespoon oil to a large non-stick frying pan/skillet over medium heat. Using a ladle, spoon the batter into the centre of the pan and use the back of the ladle to smooth it out to the edges. Add a little oil around the edge to ensure it doesn't stick.

Quickly remove the pan from the heat and scatter the top of the pancake with some of the prepared vegetable topping ingredients. Use the back of the ladle to push the vegetables slightly into the batter. Return the pan to the heat and cook for 3 minutes or until the pancake begins to brown underneath, then turn it over and cook for a further 1–2 minutes. Repeat to make the remaining pancakes. Serve immediately with the suggested accompaniments.

KOREAN MOONG PANCAKES WITH PORK

These savoury pancakes often contain kimchi, the Korean spiced pickled cabbage that is becoming increasingly popular around the world, but this version uses green beans instead. Either way, they make a delicious light bite.

400 g/2 cups dried moong dal (skinned and split mung beans), soaked overnight

2 tbsp soy sauce, plus extra to serve

4 garlic cloves, crushed

1 tbsp grated fresh ginger

4 tbsp vegetable oil

250 g/8 oz. minced/ground lean pork

1 tsp salt

1 leek, trimmed and finely chopped

125 g/4 oz. green beans, fresh or frozen, chopped into small pieces

chopped pickled cucumber and sliced red chilli/chile (optional), to serve

MAKES ABOUT 12

Drain the moong dal and put them in the food processor. Blend them finely, then add 400 ml/1⅔ cups water, the soy sauce, all but 1 of the crushed garlic cloves and all but ½ teaspoon of the grated ginger. Process the mixture to a smooth purée. Transfer the moong dal purée to a bowl, then leave the batter to sit for at least 30 minutes.

Meanwhile, heat 2 tablespoons of the oil in a frying pan/skillet or wok and fry the remaining garlic for 1 minute before adding the pork, together with the remaining ½ teaspoon of grated ginger and salt. Stir well and continue to cook until the pork is cooked through, then add the chopped leek and green beans and continue to cook gently until the vegetables are al dente. Take off the heat and set aside.

Heat a teaspoon of oil in a non-stick frying pan over a medium heat, and when it is hot, pour a spoonful of the batter into the pan. Spread out the batter with the back of the ladle until it forms a 8-cm/3-inch circle. Repeat the process with more batter, frying several pancakes at once.

Cook the pancakes until golden brown on the underside and until tiny holes have begun to appear on the upper surface, then flip them over and cook the other side. This will probably take about 5 minutes on each side. It is important not to overheat the pan and burn the surface before the inside is cooked, but it must be hot enough for the pancakes to brown and crisp.

Keep warm while you make the other pancakes, brushing the frying pan or wok with oil before cooking each batch. Serve straight away with a bowl of soy sauce for dipping, and pickled cucumber and some sliced red chilli, if desired.

ROLLS & PANCAKES

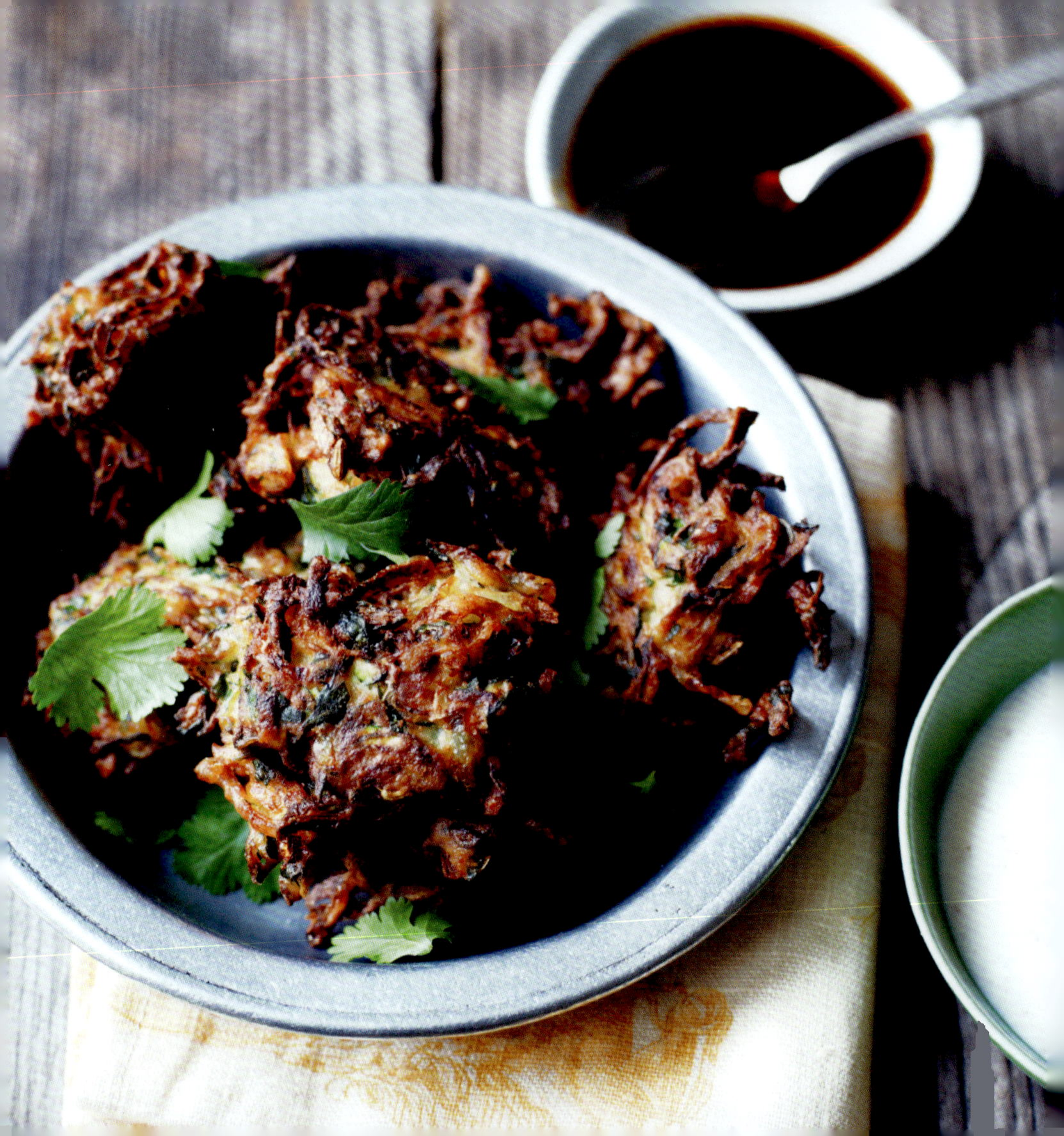

FRITTERS & FRIED SNACKS

CHANNA DHAL FRITTERS

200 g/1 cup channa dhal, picked and rinsed, then soaked in 750 ml/3¼ cups boiling water for 4 hours

½ tsp fine sea salt

1 tsp peeled and grated fresh ginger

1 tsp chopped green chillies/chiles

¼ tsp asafoetida powder

½ tsp ground turmeric

5–6 fresh coriander/cilantro stems, roughly chopped

¼ onion, finely chopped

vegetable oil, for deep-frying, plus extra for greasing

your favourite chutney or dipping sauce, to serve

MAKES 10

Channa dhal fritters make a great snack or appetizer. They consist of a spiced lentil mixture that is formed into small patties and deep-fried. The beauty of these fritters is that the outer layer becomes crispy whilst the inner part remains soft and moreish.

Drain the soaked dhal and discard the soaking water. Remove 2 heaped tablespoons of the soaked dhal and set aside in a bowl until required.

Using a food processor, blitz together the remaining channa dhal until all of the lentils are coarsely blended and form a paste. Add up to 5 tablespoons of cold water (one at a time) while the mixture is blending, if needed, to help process the mixture. Set aside.

Heat the vegetable oil for deep-frying in a deep-fat fryer or large, heavy-based saucepan to 180°C (350°F).

Meanwhile, transfer the blended lentil paste to a mixing bowl and add all the rest of the ingredients, including the reserved whole dhal. Mix well to form a thick fritter batter.

Grease your hands with a little cold oil and then shape the mixture into 10 equally-sized fritters, roughly about 5–6 cm/2–2½ inches in diameter, 1.5 cm/⅝ inch in height and weighing about 55 g/2 oz. each. A good tip is to shape them into balls to start with, then flatten each one a little between your palms so that they look like patties; slightly thicker in the middle.

Check that the oil is hot enough by dropping in a teaspoon of the mixture; if it stays in one lump and rises to the surface, then it means the oil is ready. One by one, carefully lower about half of the fritters into the hot oil, ensuring they are not touching. Don't be tempted to touch the fritters until they have turned golden and sealed all over, otherwise this may cause breakage. Deep-fry the fritters for about 10–12 minutes, turning 4–5 times, until they are evenly golden brown and crunchy.

Drain the fritters on paper towels and deep-fry the remaining batch.

Serve the fritters warm with chutney or a dipping sauce.

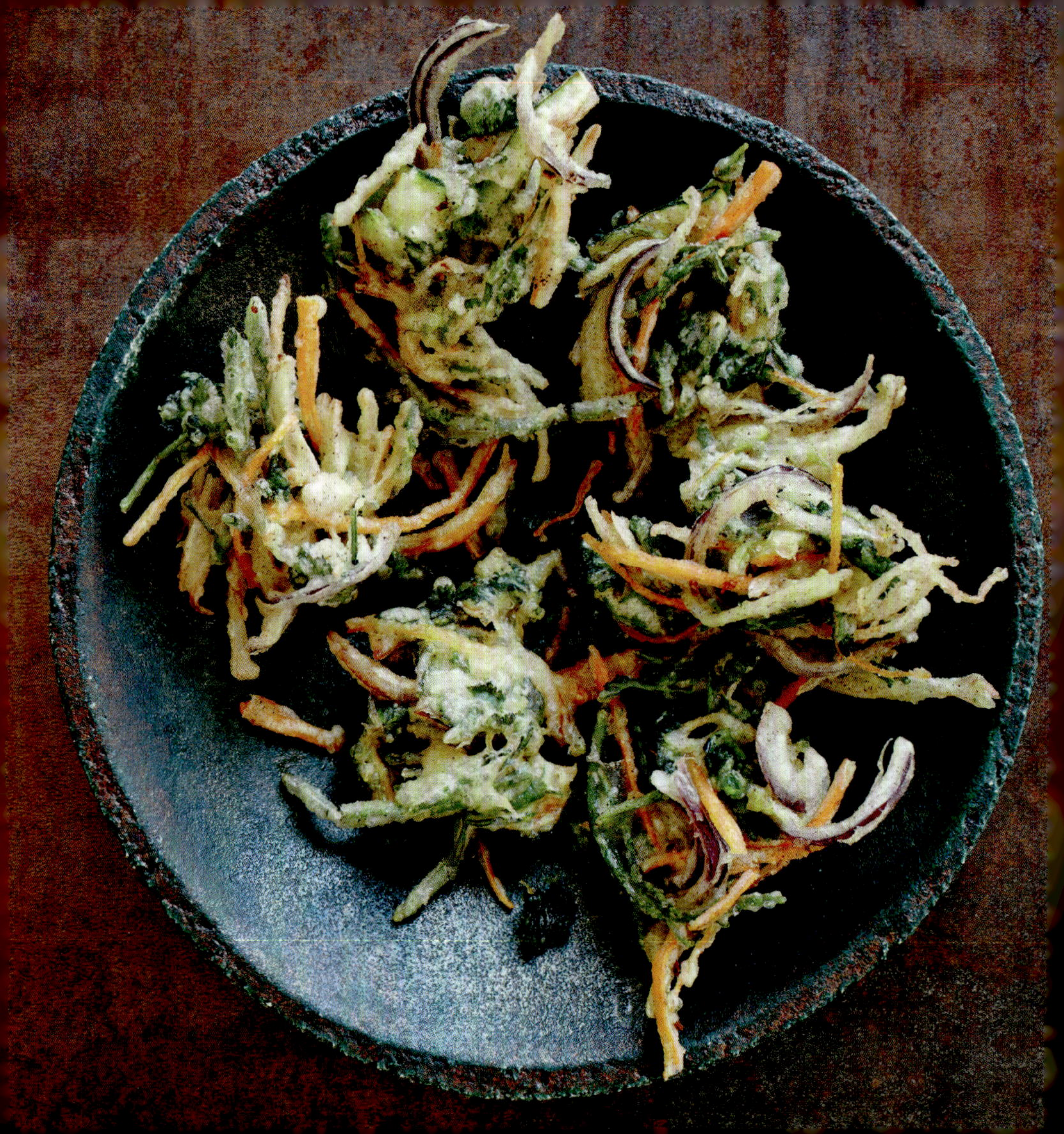

KAKIAGE PANCAKES

200 g/1½ cups self-raising/self-rising flour

200 g/2 cups cornflour/cornstarch

large pinch of salt, to season

400–500 ml/1¾ –2 cups very cold sparkling water

1 red onion, finely sliced

1 carrot, finely sliced or grated/shredded

burdock root (or salsify), finely sliced

a small bunch of spring onions/scallions

1 sweet potato

vegetable oil, for deep-frying

ponzu sauce or any other Asian dipping sauce, to serve

MAKES 10–15

Kakiage pancakes are a very simple yet comforting and delicious street-food found all over Japan. They must be served freshly cooked to retain their crispness and the coating of batter only needs to be extremely light.

To make the pancake batter, put the dry ingredients into a large mixing bowl and slowly whisk in the very cold sparkling water until you get a nice smooth, thick pancake batter with a dropping consistency.

Place the vegetables in a large bowl and mix with just enough batter to bind them all together.

Preheat the vegetable oil in a deep-fryer to 180°C (350°F) or fill a large heavy-based pan half-full with vegetable oil and heat until a cube of bread sizzles and rises to the surface instantly. Dip a dessert spoon briefly into the hot oil then pick up a portion of the battered vegetables with the same spoon and drop it carefully into the fryer.

Cook a few pancakes at a time for 2–3 minutes until golden, turning halfway. Remove with a slotted spoon and drain on paper towels. Repeat with the remaining batter and serve the hot pancakes immediately with ponzu sauce or any Asian dipping sauce.

FRITTERS & FRIED SNACKS

COURGETTE ONION BHAJIS
WITH SUMAC YOGURT & POMEGRANATE MOLASSES

This stellar twist on the classic Indian dish is the perfect way to use up those few extra courgettes/zucchini that you might have left over.

SUMAC YOGURT

250 g/1 cup Greek yogurt

1 tbsp pure maple syrup

1 tsp sumac

sea salt

BHAJIS

450 g/1 lb. courgette/zucchini, coarsely grated

70 g/½ cup chickpea/gram flour

40 g/⅓ cup rice flour

2.5-cm/1-inch piece of fresh ginger, peeled and finely grated

2 garlic cloves, peeled and crushed/minced

1 tsp ground coriander

½ tsp cumin seeds

½ tsp fennel seeds

½ tsp mustard seeds

1 large or 2 small red onion(s), thinly sliced

small handful of chopped fresh coriander/cilantro, plus extra to serve

vegetable oil, for frying

2 tbsp pomegranate molasses, to serve

SERVES 4–6

First, make the sumac yogurt. In a bowl combine together the yogurt, maple syrup, sumac and a pinch of salt and set aside.

Place the grated courgette in a sieve/strainer and press firmly to remove as much liquid as possible, then wrap in a clean dish towel and press firmly again to dry them off.

Place the flours into a large bowl and whisk in 5–6 tablespoons water to create a thick batter the consistency of double/heavy cream.

Add the ginger, garlic, spices, onion, set-aside courgette, 1 teaspoon sea salt, most of the fresh coriander and combine very well.

Pour 2.5 cm/1 inches of vegetable oil into a frying pan/skillet and set over a medium-high heat. If you have a cooking thermometer, it should be 180°C (350°F), if not test that the heat is right by dropping in a tiny amount of batter – if it turns golden and crisp after about 40 seconds it's ready.

Carefully place separate heaped tablespoons of the mixture into the hot oil, shaping into circular mounds. Do not overcrowd the pan as it will bring the temperature of the oil down.

Fry, turning once or twice until crisp and golden. Remove and drain on paper towels. Keep the cooked bhajis warm in a low oven while you fry the rest.

Serve immediately with the extra coriander sprinkled on top. Dollop the sumac yogurt and pomegranate molasses generously over each crispy bite.

FRITTERS & FRIED SNACKS

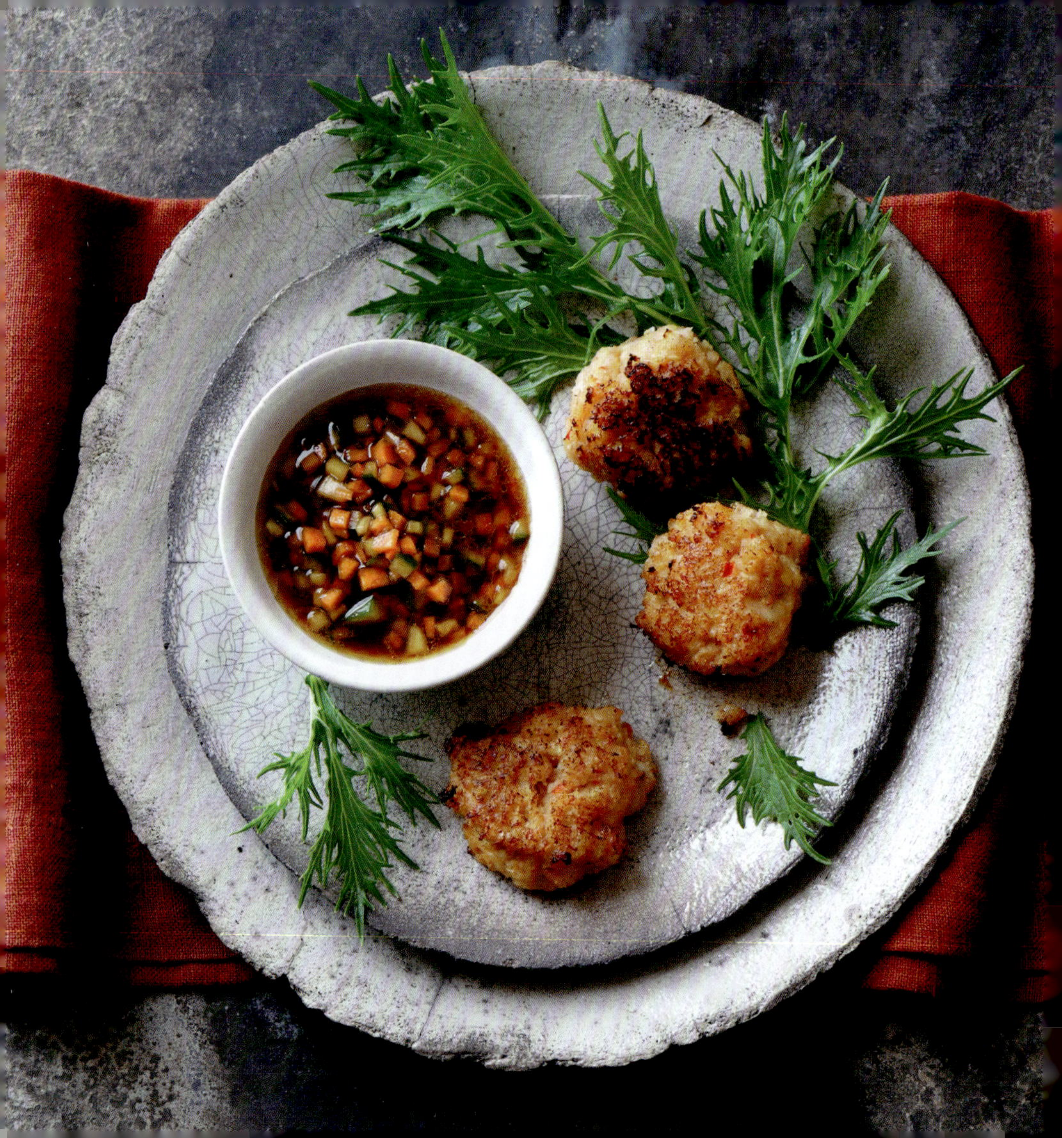

THAI FISHCAKES

Alter the amount of chilli/chile in these little Thai bites to suit your personal spice preferences. Add more if you like a kick.

3 garlic cloves, peeled
1 red chilli/chile
2 onions, chopped
1 tsp chilli/chile powder
½ tsp ground cumin
½ tsp ground coriander
50 g/5 tbsp fresh ginger, peeled and grated
1 tsp tamarind paste
grated zest and juice of 1 lime
2 tbsp fish sauce
400 g/14 oz. white fish fillet (such as hake, pollock, whiting or cod), chopped into 2-cm/¾-inch pieces
vegetable oil, for frying

DIPPING SAUCE
2 tbsp brown sugar
1 tbsp dark soy sauce
2 tbsp sesame oil
1 tbsp fish sauce
juice of 1 lime
½ carrot, finely diced
½ cucumber, finely diced

SERVES 4

Begin by making the dipping sauce. Heat the sugar, soy sauce, sesame oil and fish sauce in a saucepan set over a medium heat. Remove from the heat and let cool, before adding the lime juice, carrot and cucumber. Set aside until ready to serve.

Put the garlic, chilli and onions in a food processor or blender and pulse until finely chopped and combined. Add the spices, ginger, tamarind, lime zest and juice and fish sauce, and pulse again to combine. Finally, add the fish pieces and pulse briefly until fully combined – it should be the texture of a thick porridge. Don't over-blend the mixture once the fish has been added as it can easily become a paste.

Heat a little vegetable oil in a saucepan set over a medium heat. Scoop tablespoonfuls of the mixture into the hot pan. After about a minute, flip the fishcakes over and cook for a further minute, until golden brown. Serve warm with the dipping sauce.

CRISPY CHICKEN WONTONS

1 chicken breast fillet (approx. 140 g/5 oz.), finely minced/ground

4 tbsp finely chopped Chinese chives

pinch of ground Sichuan pepper

1 tsp light soy sauce

½ tsp sesame oil

16 wonton wrappers

sunflower or vegetable oil, for deep frying

salt and black pepper

DIPPING SAUCE

2 tbsp Chinese black rice vinegar

1 tsp sugar

1 garlic clove, finely chopped

½ red chilli/chile, finely chopped (optional)

MAKES 16

Deep-frying these dumplings until they are crisp transforms them into an appetizing snack. When served with the dipping sauce, they go perfectly with pre-dinner drinks.

Thoroughly mix together the chicken, chives, Sichuan pepper, soy sauce and sesame oil. Season well with salt and pepper.

Mix together the ingredients for the dipping sauce and set aside.

Take a wonton wrapper and place a teaspoon of the chicken mixture in the centre of the wrapper. Brush the edges with a little cold water and bring the wrapper together over the chicken to form a parcel, pressing together well to seal properly. Set aside. Repeat the process until all 16 wrappers have been filled.

Heat the oil in a large saucepan or deep-fryer until very hot. Add four of the wontons and fry for a few minutes, until golden brown on both sides, turning over halfway through to ensure even browning. Remove with a slotted spoon and drain on paper towels. Repeat the process with the remaining wontons.

Serve at once with the dipping sauce.

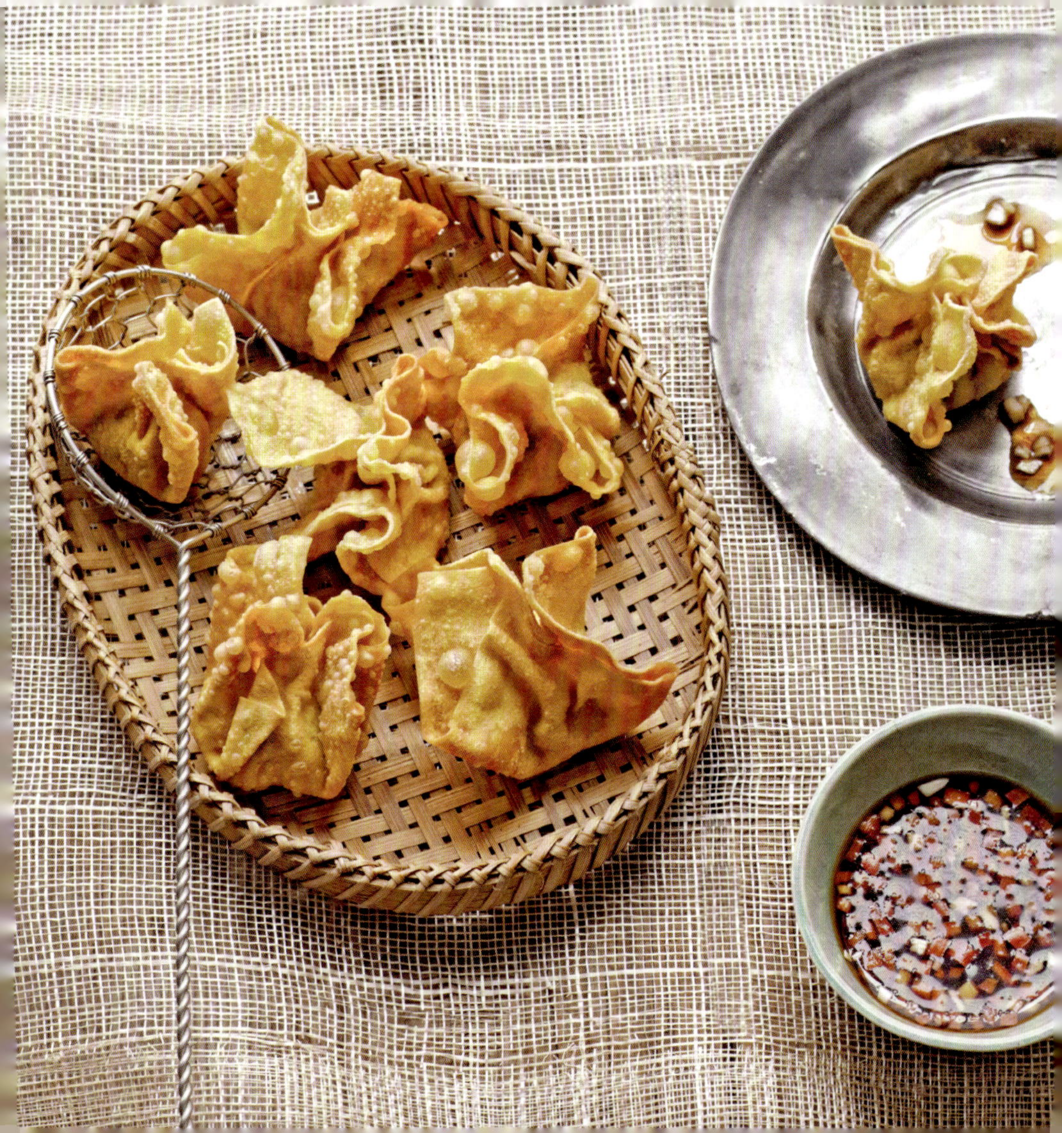

SESAME PRAWN TOASTS WITH PICKLED CARROT

Dishes that can be made ahead of time are very useful – especially if you serve these when entertaining! This prawn mixture can be 'prepped' several hours in advance and the toasts cooked to order.

300 g/10 oz. uncooked prawns/shrimp, shelled and deveined

6 spring onions/scallions, thinly sliced

1 tbsp fresh ginger, peeled and grated

2 tsp dry sherry (optional)

1 tsp light soy sauce

1 egg white, lightly beaten

6 thick slices of white bread

50 g/⅓ cup sesame seeds

about 250 ml/1 cup vegetable oil, for shallow-frying

sprigs of fresh coriander/cilantro, to garnish

salt, to season

PICKLED CARROT

1 large carrot, coarsely grated

2 tbsp Japanese pickled ginger, sliced

2 tbsp juice from the pickled ginger jar

½ tsp caster/granulated sugar

2 shallots, thinly sliced on a diagonal

MAKES 24

To make the pickled carrot, combine the carrot, pickled ginger, pickled ginger juice, sugar and shallots in a small, non-reactive bowl. Set aside until needed.

Put the prawns, spring onions, ginger, sherry, soy sauce, egg white and some salt in a food processor or blender. Process until roughly chopped.

Trim the crusts off the bread and discard or save for another use. Cut each slice into 4 triangles.

Put the sesame seeds on a plate.

Spread about 2 teaspoons of the prawn mixture onto each piece of bread, pressing down lightly.

Press each triangle into the sesame seeds to lightly coat.

Put the oil in a shallow frying pan/skillet and heat over a medium-high heat. Add a piece of bread to test if the oil is ready – if the bread sizzles on contact, the oil is hot enough. Use a fish slice to carefully add the prawn toasts to the pan, prawn-side down, and cook for 1 minute. Turn over and cook for 1 minute more, until golden. Drain on paper towels.

Spoon a little pickled carrot over the top of each toast and add a sprig of coriander. Serve immediately.

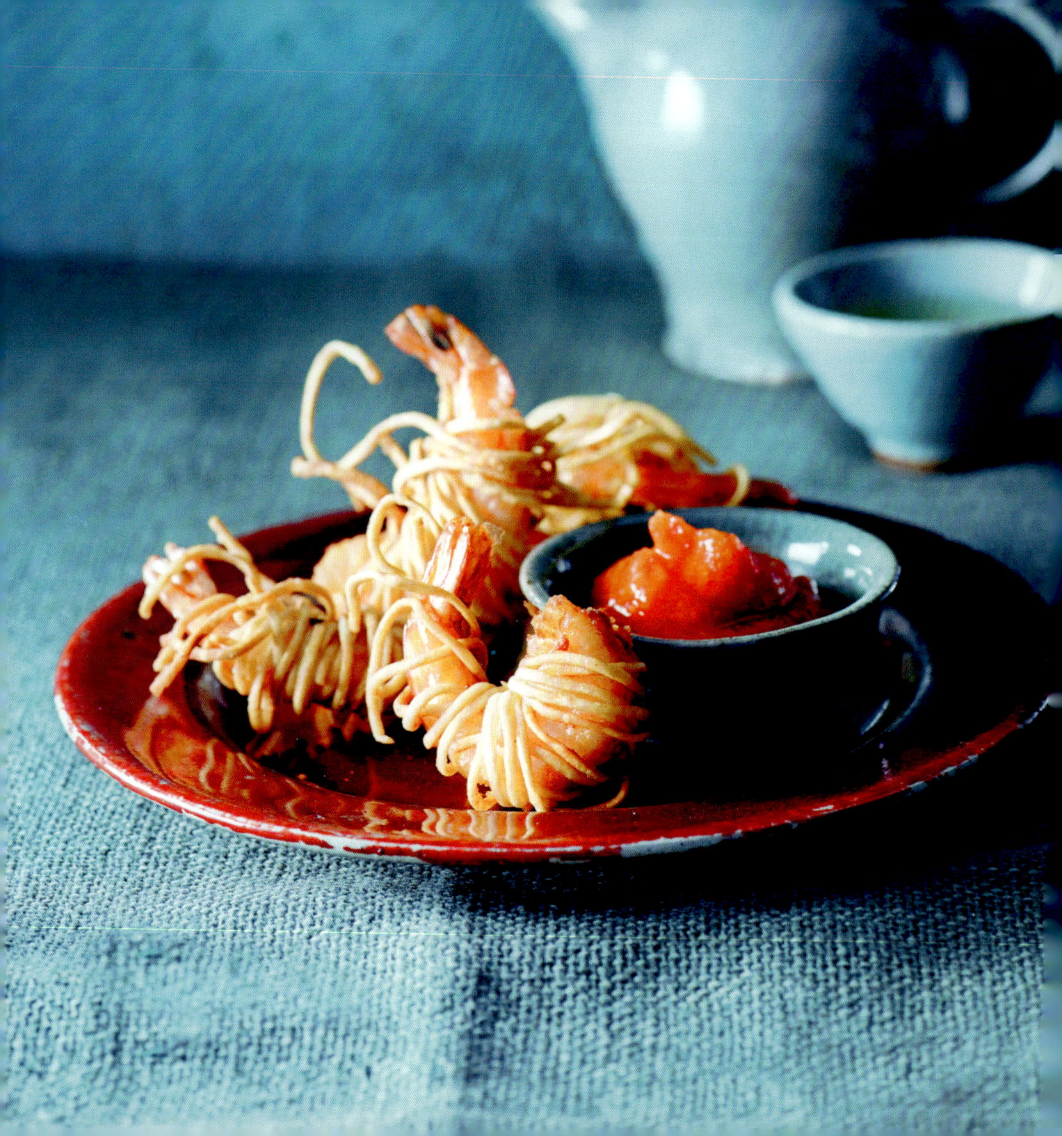

PRAWNS WRAPPED IN NOODLES
WITH SWEET CHILLI/CHILE SAUCE

These bite-sized snacks make lovely canapés or finger food.

100 g/3½ oz. dried thin egg noodles

24 large uncooked prawns/shrimp, shelled and deveined

vegetable oil, for deep-frying

sweet chilli/chile sauce, to serve

a baking sheet lined with baking parchment

SERVES 4

Put the noodles in a bowl, cover with boiling water and soak for 20 minutes until softened. Drain the noodles and pat dry with paper towels. Wrap 8–10 noodles around each prawn and set aside.

Preheat the oven to 110°C (225°F) Gas ¼ (or the lowest heat setting).

Pour vegetable oil into a wok or large saucepan to reach about 5 cm/2 inches up the side and set over a medium-high heat. Heat until a cube of bread dropped into the oil crisps in 30 seconds.

Deep-fry the wrapped prawns in batches for 2–3 minutes until the noodles are crisp and prawns are cooked through.

Turn off the oven and set aside the cooked prawns in the still-warm oven while you cook the remaining prawns in the same way.

Serve with the sweet chilli sauce.

PRAWN & MANGO WONTONS

Deep-fried crispy wontons are a moreish pleasure to eat. The tropical mango dipping sauce provides a sweet and sharp tang to cut through the savouriness of the skin.

350 g/12½ oz. raw prawns/shrimp, peeled and deveined

1 tsp salt

1 tsp black pepper

small handful of chopped fresh coriander/cilantro

50 g/1¾ oz. firm tofu, drained and sliced, excess water pressed out

16 wonton wrappers

sunflower oil, for deep-frying

DIPPING SAUCE

4 tablepoons mayonnaise

2 tsp condensed milk

¼ small mango, diced into small cubes

MAKES 16

Use a pestle and mortar to mince the prawns to a fine paste. Season with the salt and pepper and mix in the coriander. Mash the tofu with a fork and add to the paste, stirring in well.

Hold a wonton skin on the palm of your hand and add a heaped teaspoon of filling to the centre. Dab the edges of the skin with a tiny bit of water and gather and scrunch the sides together in a rustic fashion. Repeat until all the filling and skins are used.

Heat the oil in a deep-fryer or large pan until it reaches 180°C/350°F. Cook the wontons in the hot oil in small batches for around a minute on either side. The wontons are cooked when they float up and the skins have turned golden brown. Drain the excess oil on paper towels.

To make dipping sauce, sweeten the mayonnaise with the condensed milk and stir in the diced mango. Serve the wontons hot with the mango dipping sauce.

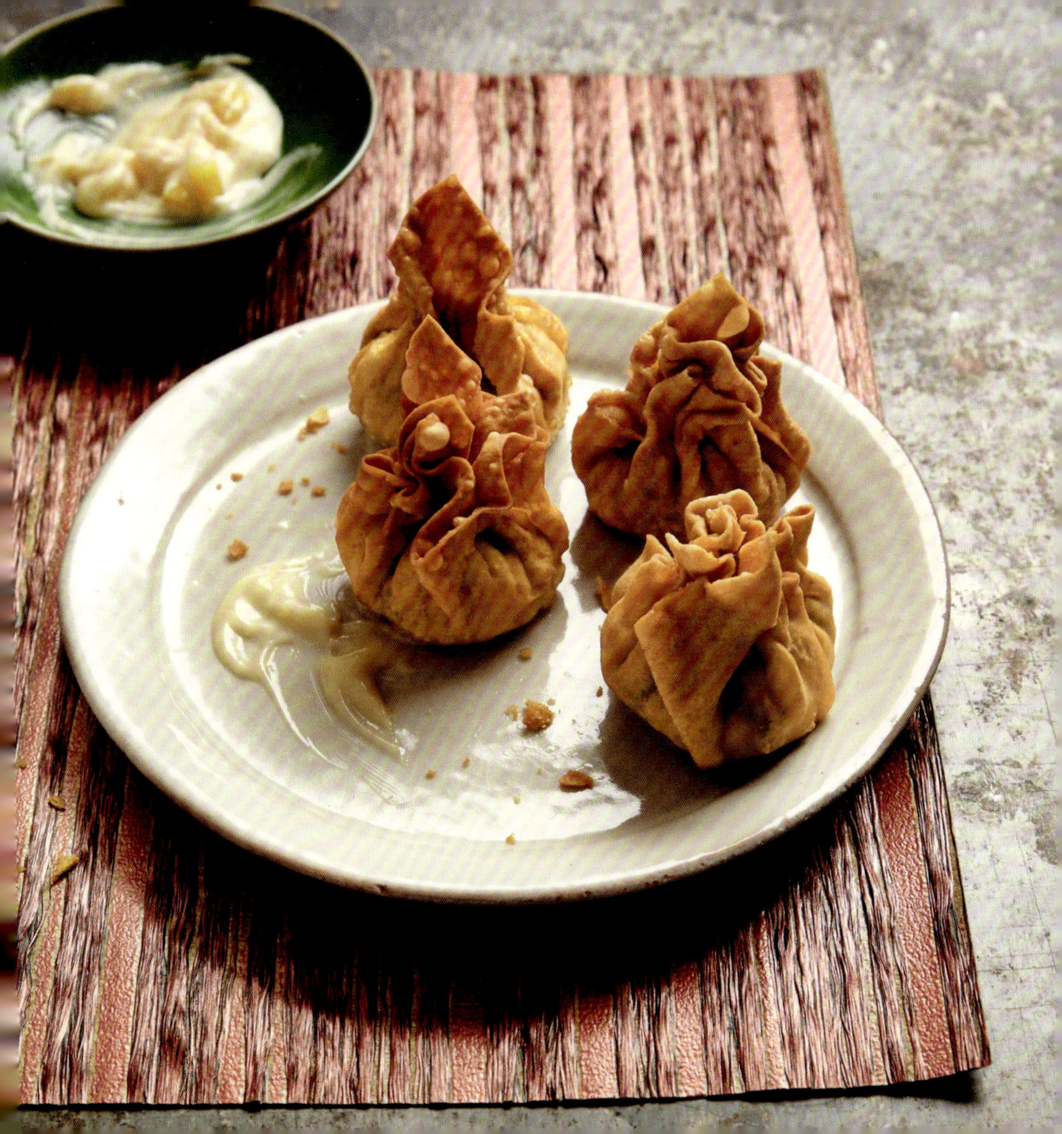

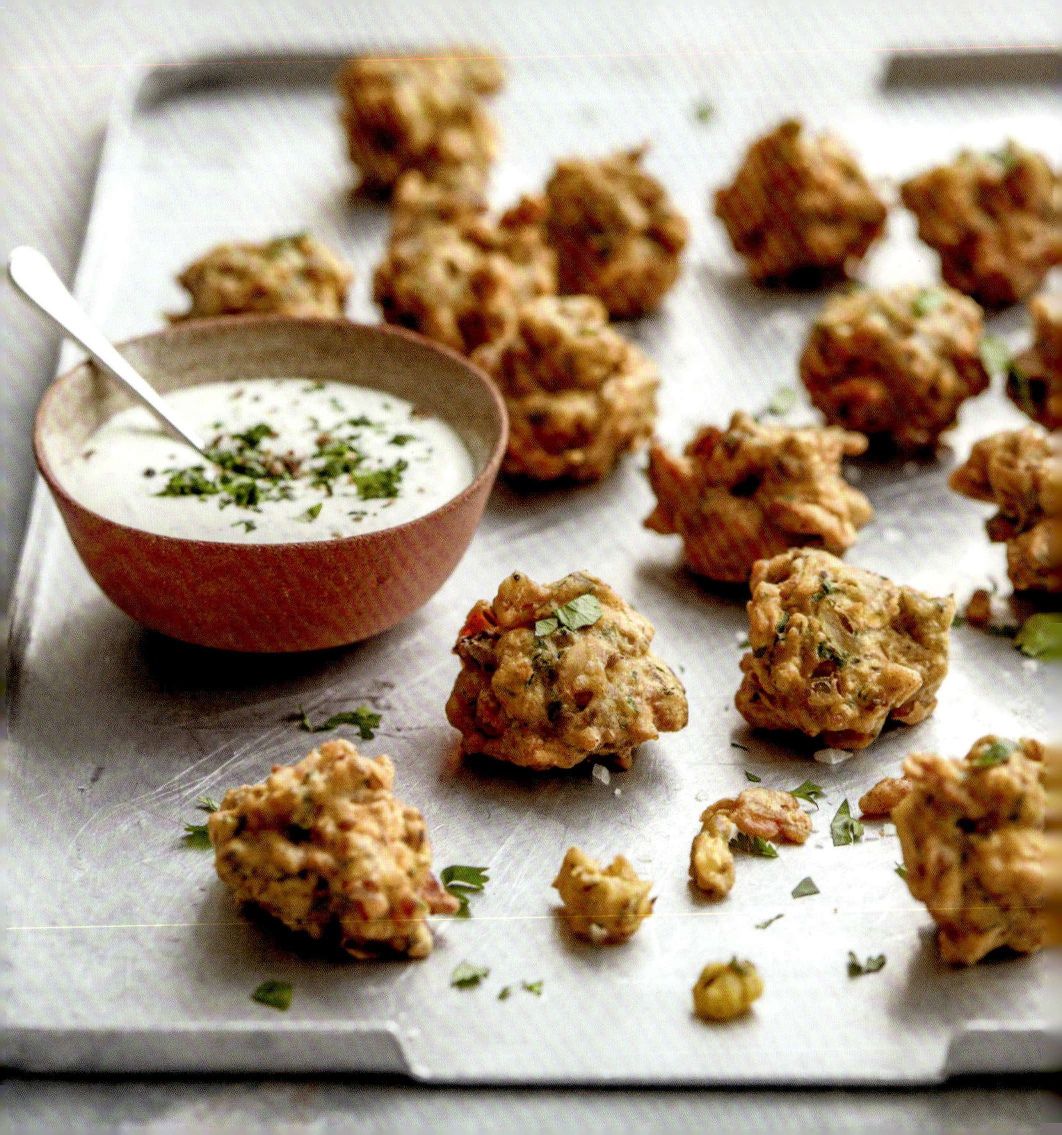

MUSHROOM PAKORAS

115 g/¾ cup chickpea/gram flour

1 tsp ground cumin

1 tsp cumin seeds

½ tsp ground turmeric

½ tsp salt

½ tsp baking powder

½ onion, chopped

200 g/6½ oz. mushrooms, chopped

2–3 sprigs chopped fresh coriander/cilantro

vegetable oil, for deep-frying

lemon wedges, to serve (optional)

YOGURT DIP

4 tbsp chopped fresh coriander/cilantro or mint

200 ml/1 scant cup plain/natural yogurt

MAKES ABOUT 12–14

There is something irresistible about deep-fried food! These Indian pakoras – made with nutty-tasting chickpea/gram flour and flavoured with fragrant spices – are ideal for a drinks party served alongside other Indian small plates. Serve with a herbed yogurt dipping sauce or simply with lemon wedges.

First, make the yogurt dip. Stir the chopped coriander or mint into the yogurt and set aside.

Place the chickpea flour, ground cumin and seeds, turmeric, salt and baking powder in a mixing bowl. Whisk in 120 ml/½ cup water to form a smooth batter. Fold in the onion, mushrooms and coriander.

Heat the oil in a wok or large frying pan/skillet until very hot. Cook the pakoras in batches, dropping in a tablespoon of the mixture for each pakora. Fry for about 3–5 minutes, until golden brown, turning over each pakora as it cooks to ensure even browning. Remove the pakoras with a slotted spoon and drain on paper towels.

Serve at once with the yogurt dip or lemon wedges for squeezing over the top.

MASALA DHAL VADAS

200 g/1 cup dried split channa dhal soaked in 600 ml/2½ cups water for 6 hours (this should yield a total of 350 g/2¼ cups)

½ tsp salt

1 tsp grated fresh root ginger

1 tsp chopped green chilli/chile

100 g/scant ½ cup mashed potatoes

¼ tsp asafoetida powder

½ tsp Kashmiri red chilli/chili powder

½ tsp garam masala

½ tsp ground turmeric

2 tbsp chopped fresh coriander/cilantro

½ onion, finely chopped

vegetable oil, for deep-frying and greasing

chutney of your choice, to serve

deep-fat fryer (optional)

SERVES 4 (MAKES 16 VADAS)

Dhal vadas make a great snack; they are made from a spiced lentil mixture that is deep-fried to form fritters. These moreish small bites have mashed potatoes added to the mixture to keep the insides irresistibly soft.

Remove 2 tablespoons of the soaked channa dhal and set aside until required. Using a food processor, blitz together the remaining channa dhal until all of the lentils have been coarsely chopped.

Combine all of the ingredients, including the dhal, in a mixing bowl and mix well to form a fritter batter. Grease your hands with a little oil and roll into 16 fritters about 30 g/1 oz. each. I shape them into balls to start with and then flatten them with the palm of my hands so that they look like patties that are slightly thicker in the middle and thinner on the edges.

Heat the oil for deep-frying in a deep-fat fryer or large, heavy-bottomed pan to 180°C (350°F). Deep-fry the fritters in batches in the hot oil until golden-brown; this should take 5–6 minutes. (The fritters should be crunchy on the outside and soft in the inside.) Drain and serve warm with your favourite chutney.

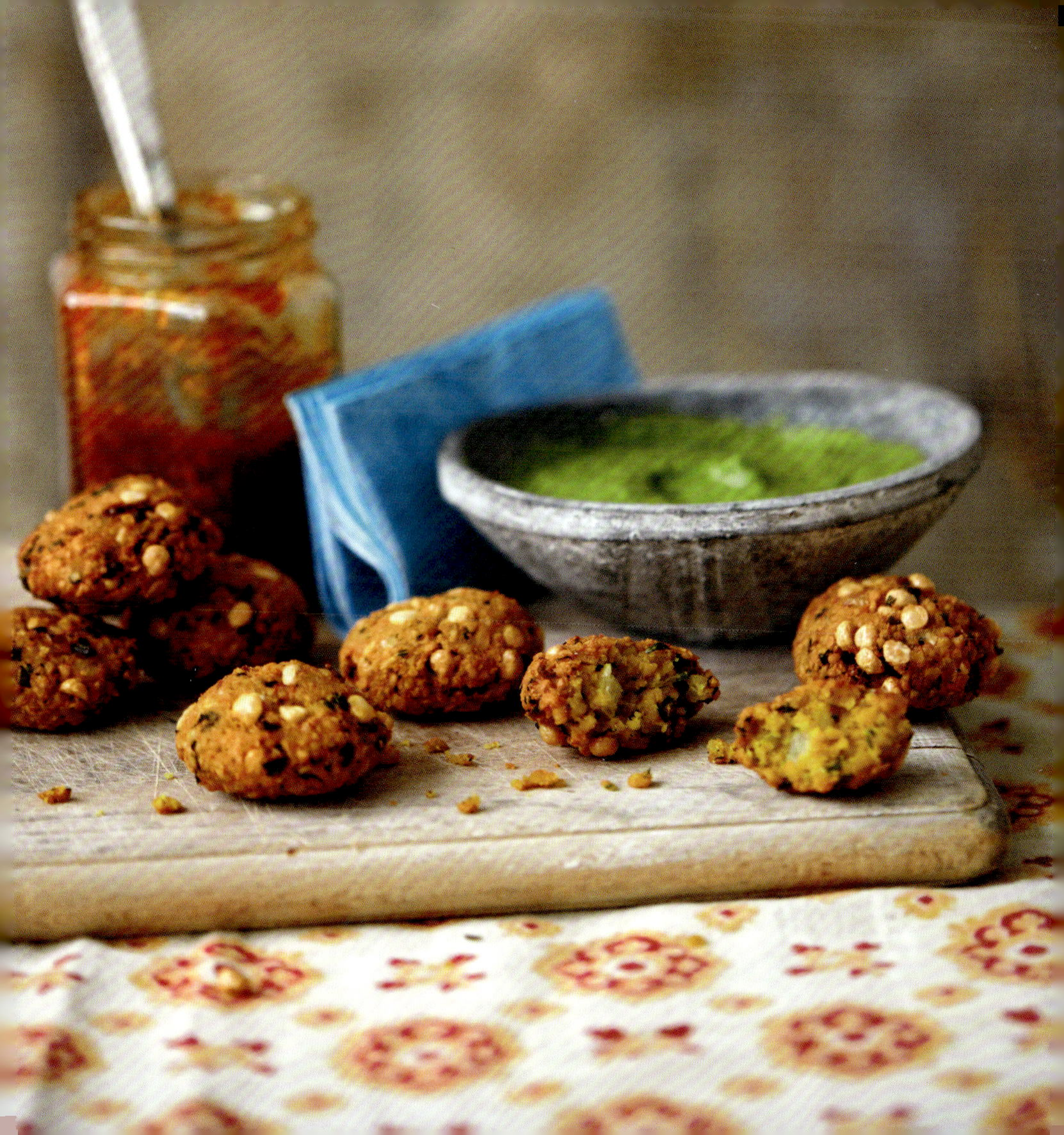

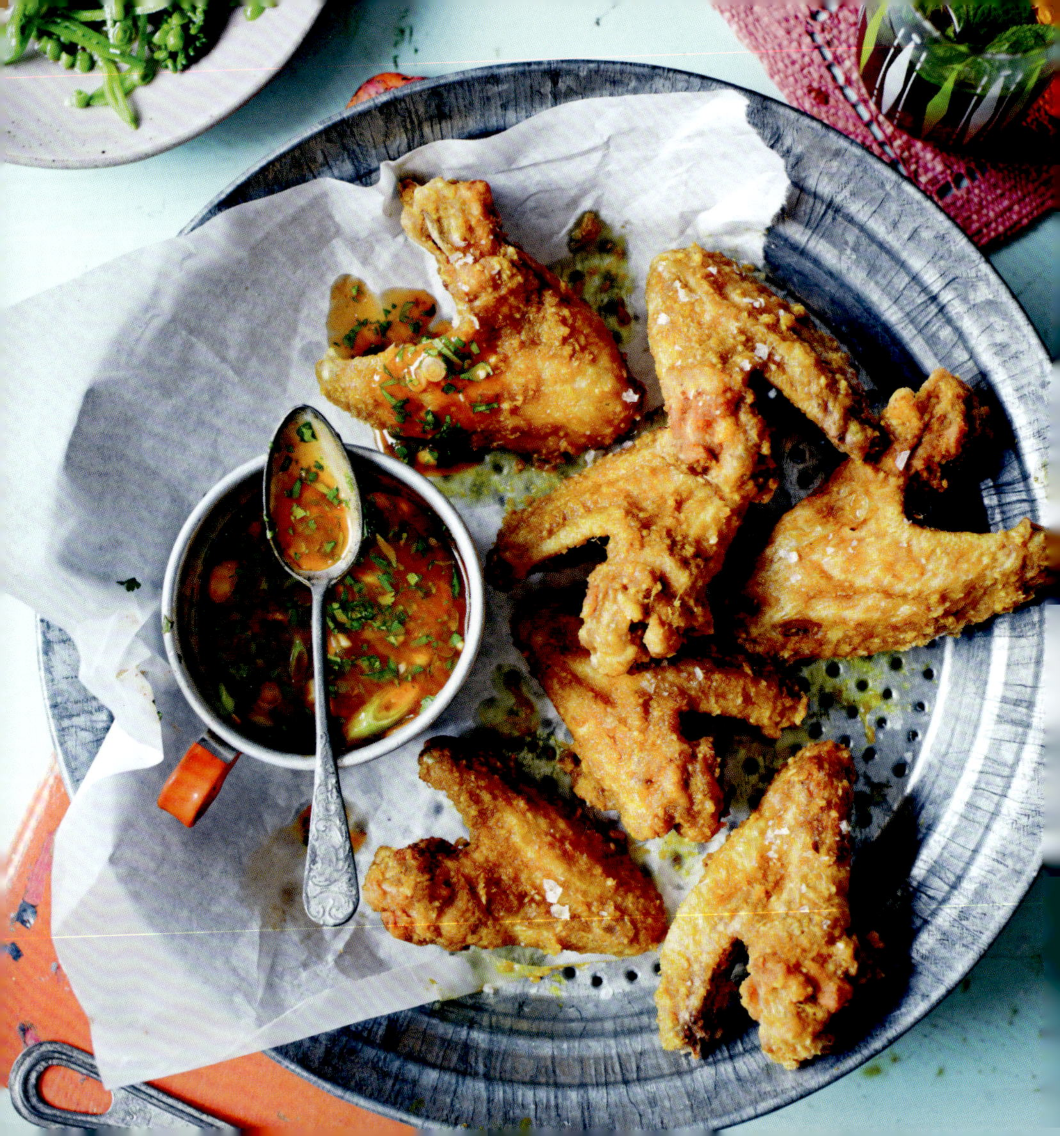

SKEWERS & WINGS

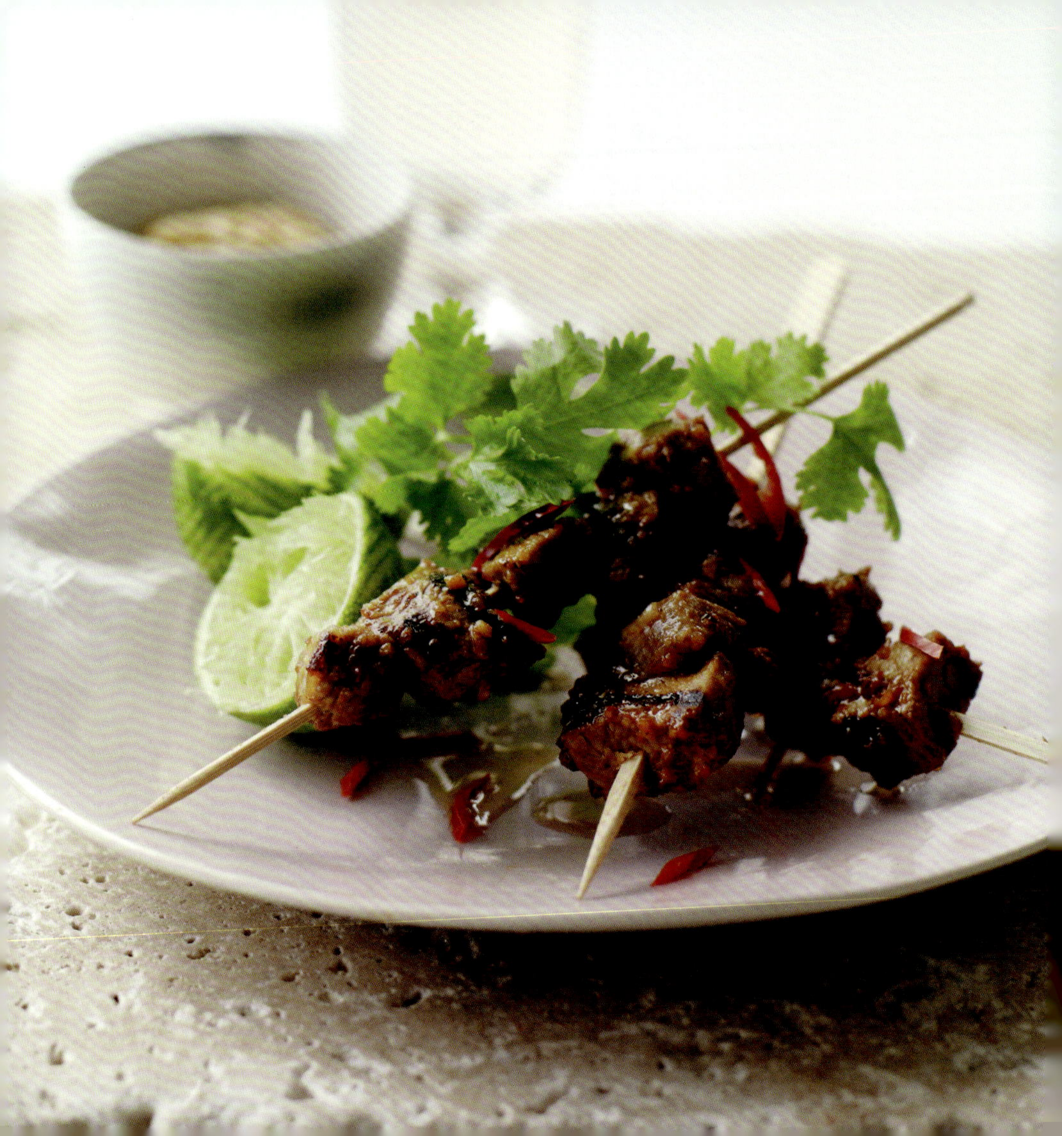

FIERY BEEF SATAY IN PEANUT SAUCE

500 g/1 lb. beef sirloin, sliced against the grain into bite-sized pieces

1 tbsp groundnut/peanut oil

PEANUT SAUCE

60 ml/¼ cup peanut or vegetable oil

4–5 garlic cloves, minced

4–5 dried serrano chillies/chiles, deseeded and ground with a pestle and mortar

1–2 tsp curry powder

60 g/½ cup roasted peanuts, finely ground

TO SERVE

a small bunch of fresh coriander/cilantro

a small bunch of fresh mint

lime wedges

a packet of short wooden or bamboo skewers, soaked in water before use

SERVES 4–6

Beef, pork or chicken satays cooked in, or served with, a fiery peanut sauce are hugely popular throughout Southeast Asia. This particular sauce is a great favourite in Thailand, Vietnam and Indonesia.

To make the sauce, heat the oil in a heavy-based saucepan and stir in the garlic until it begins to colour. Add the chillies, curry powder and the peanuts and stir over a gentle heat, until the mixture forms a paste. Remove from the heat and leave to cool.

Put the beef pieces in a bowl. Beat the oil into the sauce and tip the mixture onto the beef. Mix together well, so that the beef is evenly coated and thread the meat onto the prepared skewers.

Prepare a charcoal or conventional grill. Cook the satays for 2–3 minutes on each side, then serve the skewered meat with the fresh herbs to wrap around each tasty morsel, and lime wedges for squeezing.

DUCK SATAY WITH GRILLED PINEAPPLE & PLUM SAUCE

700 g/1 lb. 9 oz. duck breasts or boned thighs, sliced into thin, bite-sized strips

1–2 tbsp groundnut/peanut or coconut oil, for brushing

1 small pineapple, peeled, cored and sliced

Chinese plum sauce, to serve

MARINADE

2–3 tbsp light soy sauce

juice of 1 lime

1–2 tsp caster/granulated sugar

1–2 garlic cloves, crushed/minced

25 g/1 oz. fresh ginger, peeled and grated

1 small onion, grated

1–2 tsp ground coriander

1 tsp salt

a packet of wooden or bamboo skewers, soaked in water before use

SERVES 4

Chicken satays are popular throughout Southeast Asia but in Vietnam, Cambodia and China, duck satays are common too. Duck is often served in the Chinese tradition of sweet and sour with a fruity sauce.

To make the marinade, put the soy sauce and lime juice in a bowl with the sugar and mix until it dissolves. Add the garlic, ginger and grated onion and stir in the coriander and salt.

Place the strips of duck in a bowl and pour over the marinade. Toss well, cover and chill in the refrigerator for at least 4 hours.

Thread the duck strips onto the skewers and brush them with oil.

Prepare a charcoal or conventional grill/broiler.

Cook the satays for 3–4 minutes on each side, until the duck is nicely browned. Grill the slices of pineapple at the same time. When browned, cut them into bite-sized pieces and serve with the duck. Drizzle with the plum sauce to serve.

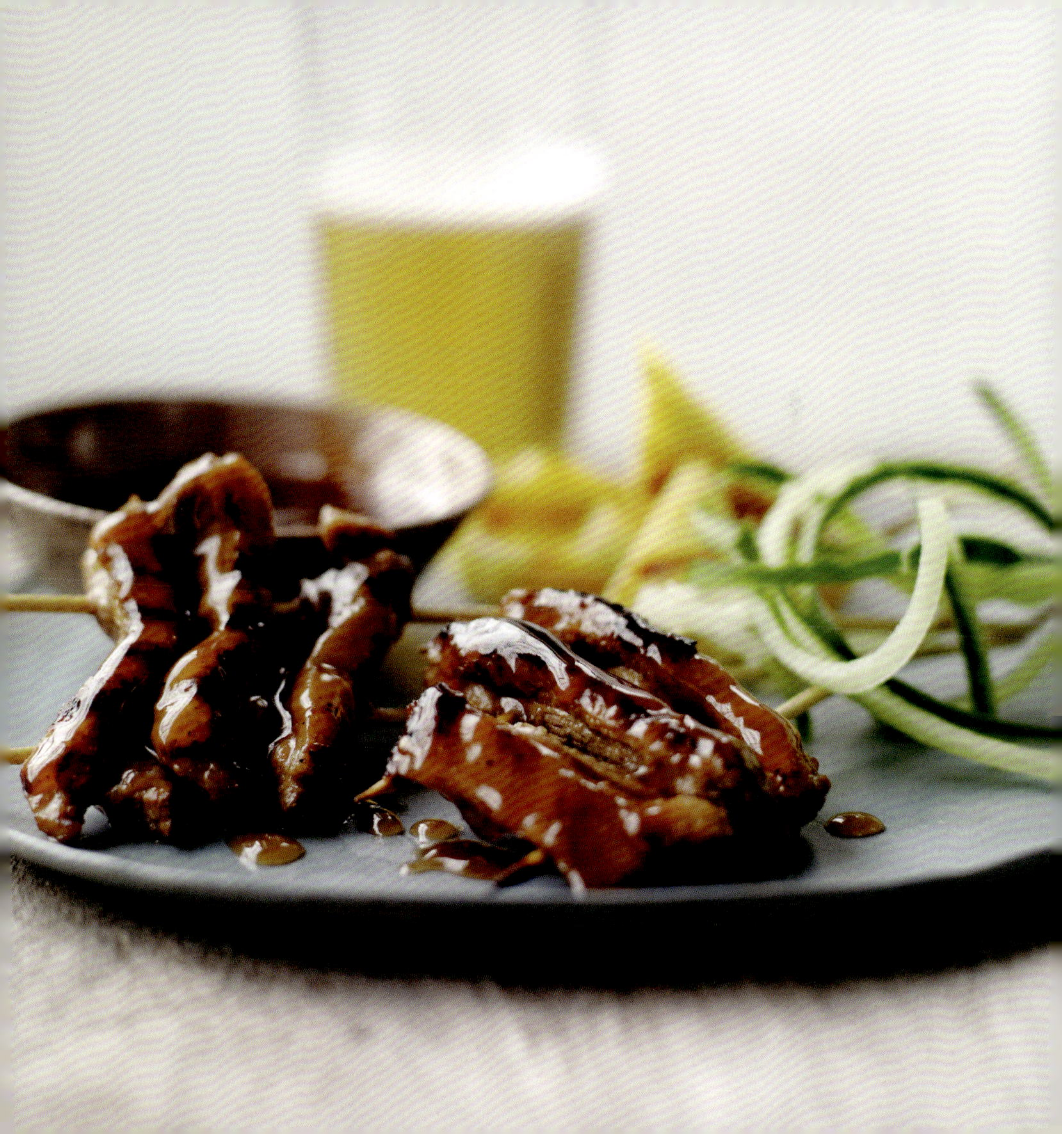

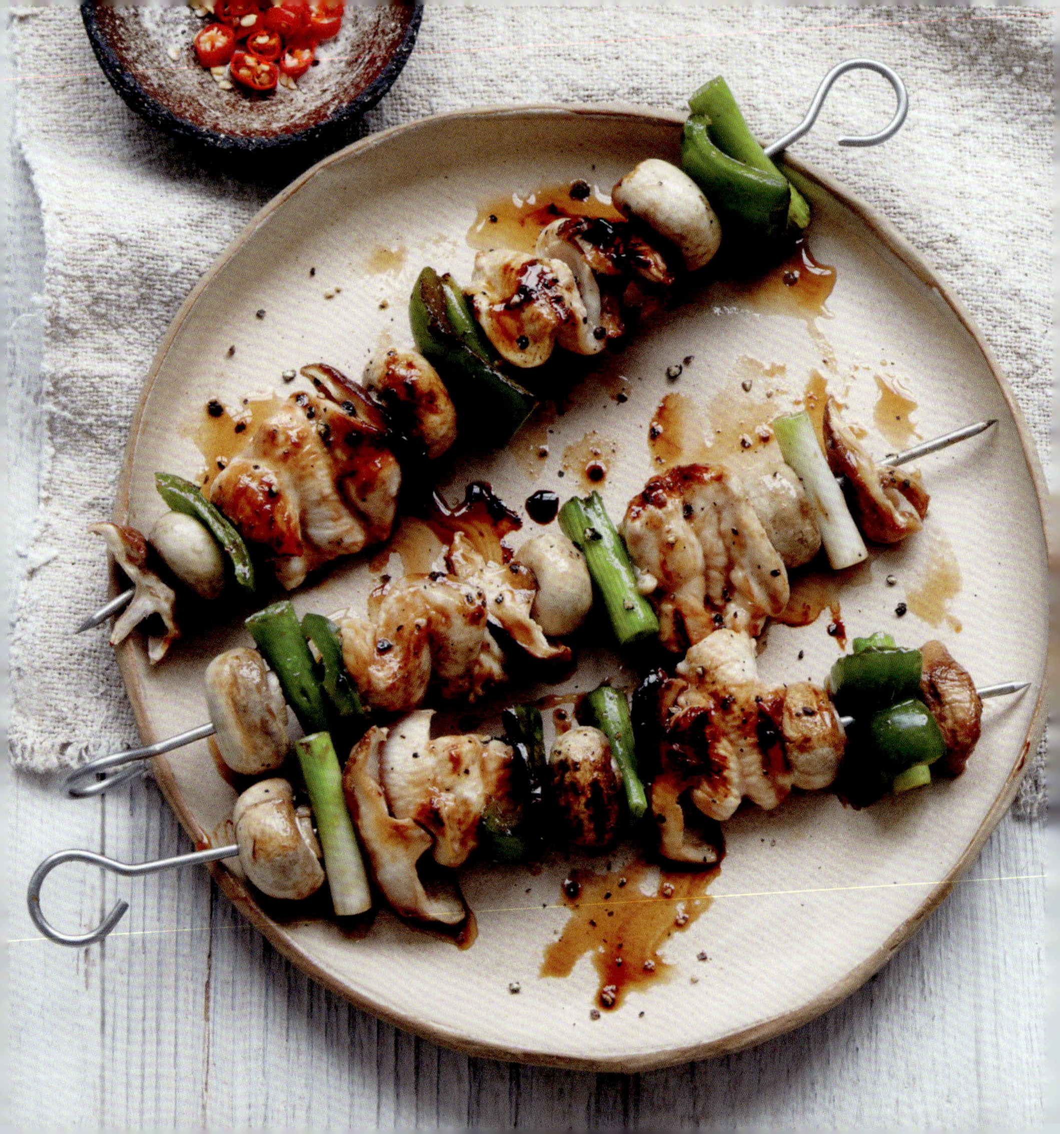

YAKITORI-GLAZED MUSHROOM & CHICKEN SKEWERS

16 white/cup mushrooms, stalks trimmed off

250 g/8 oz. boneless chicken breast, cut into thin strips

16 fresh shiitake mushrooms, halved, stalks trimmed off

½ green (bell) pepper, deseeded and cut into 2-cm/1-inch squares

2 spring onions/scallions, cut into 2-cm/¾-inch lengths

finely sliced red chilli/chile, to garnish (optional)

YAKITORI GLAZE

50 ml/3 tbsp rice wine or Amontillado sherry

50 ml/3 tbsp mirin

50 ml/3 tbsp light soy sauce

1 tbsp white granulated sugar

¼ tsp salt

8 long metal skewers

SERVES 4–6

These salty-sweet glazed chicken skewers go down well with everyone and are the perfect quick, but satisfying snack.

Make the yakitori glaze by placing the rice wine or sherry, mirin, soy sauce, sugar and salt in a small saucepan. Bring to the boil and boil for 1 minute until melted together into a syrupy glaze. Turn off the heat.

Thread the mushrooms, chicken, shiitake mushrooms, green (bell) pepper and spring onion onto the skewers.

Preheat the grill/broiler to high. Brush the prepared skewers generously with the yakitori glaze. Grill/broil the skewers for 8–10 minutes, until the chicken is cooked through, brushing repeatedly with the glaze and turning the skewers over halfway through.

Sprinkle with some sliced chilli if liked and serve at once.

THAI-STYLE FRIED CHICKEN WINGS

Let's be honest, for some fried chicken isn't so much of a craze as it is a way of life. This recipe is spicy, crispy, full of Thai flavours and perfect for Friday night snacks.

vegetable or canola oil, for frying

9 garlic cloves

7.5-cm/3-inch piece of fresh ginger, peeled

6 tbsp soy sauce

6 tbsp curry paste

3 tbsp rice vinegar

2 tbsp coconut oil, melted

2 tbsp runny honey

180 g/1⅓ cups plain/all-purpose flour

2 tbsp cornflour/cornstarch

1.8 kg/4 lb. chicken wings, halved at the joints, tips removed

LEMONGRASS & SOY DIPPING SAUCE

3 stalks of lemongrass

2 spring onions/scallions, chopped

1 tsp finely chopped garlic

1 tsp brown sugar

1 tbsp sriracha sauce

3 tbsp lime juice

1 tbsp fish sauce

2 tsp soy sauce

1 tbsp chopped fresh coriander/cilantro

1 tbsp chopped fresh basil

SERVES 4–6

First, make the dipping sauce. Trim the end of the lemongrass stalks and remove the outer layers, then finely chop. Place in a bowl with the other ingredients and 3 tablespoons water. Mix well, then cover and chill in the refrigerator until ready to serve.

Preheat the oil in the deep-fat fryer or a deep saucepan to 180°C (350°F).

Chop the garlic and ginger by pulsing briefly in a food processor. Add the soy sauce, curry paste, vinegar, coconut oil and honey. Purée until smooth. Transfer the sauce to a bowl.

In a separate bowl, whisk the flour and cornflour with 350 ml/1⅔ cups water. Add the chicken and toss until well coated.

Fry the chicken in about three batches for 6–8 minutes until golden, then drain on paper towels.

Bring the oil back to 180°C (350°F) and fry the chicken for a further 6–8 minutes, until crisp and the juices run clear when the thickest part is pierced to the bone. Drain again, then toss the chicken in the sauce.

Serve with the lemongrass and soy dipping sauce.

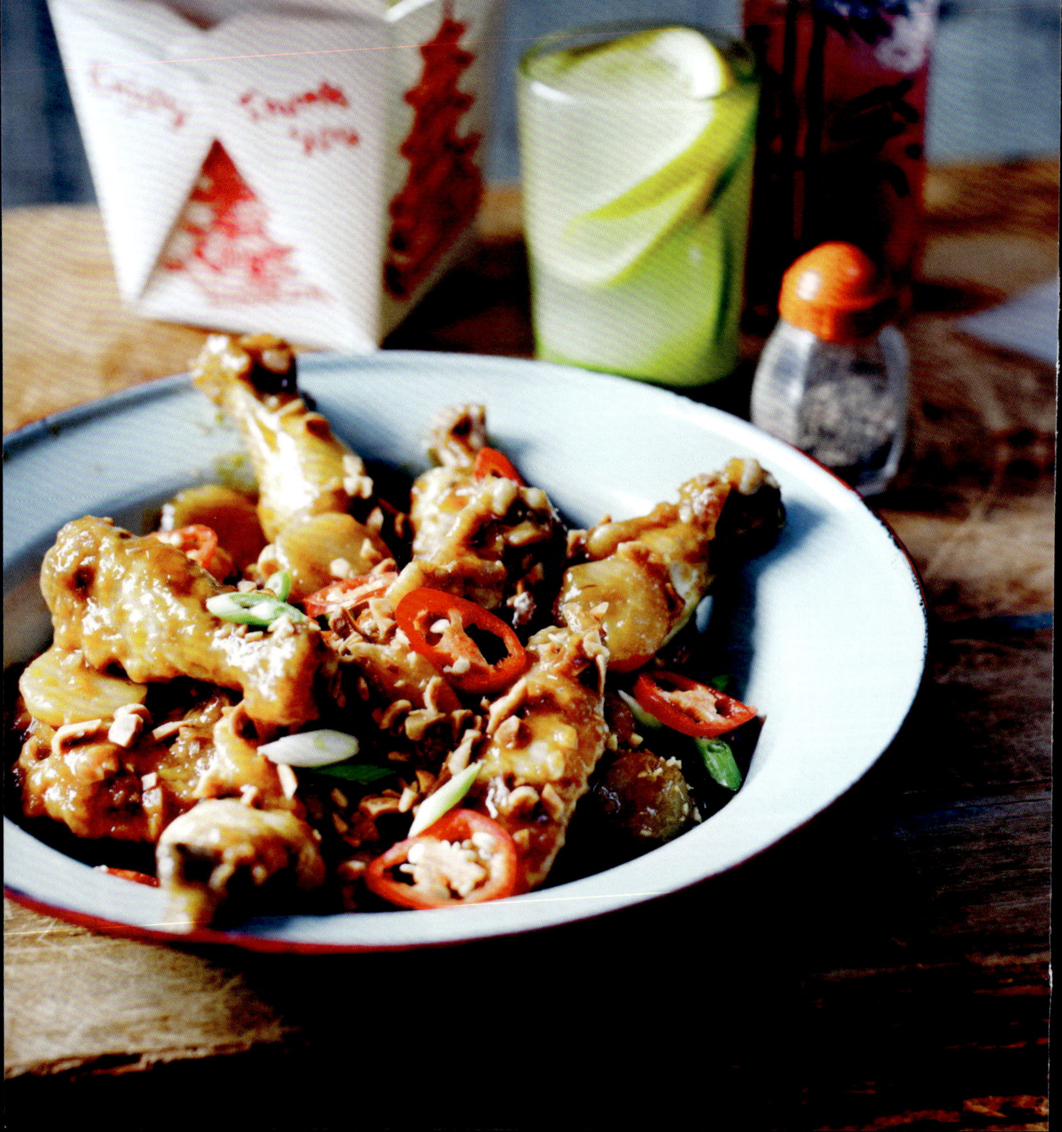

KUNG PAO WINGS

120 ml/½ cup white wine

120 ml/½ cup soy sauce

4 tbsp sesame oil,

50 g/½ cup cornflour/cornstarch, dissolved in 120 ml/½ cup water

1.8 kg/4 lb. chicken wings, halved at the joints, tips removed

85 g/3 oz. hot chilli/chile paste

1½ tbsp distilled white vinegar

3 tbsp brown sugar

4 spring onions/scallions, chopped, plus extra to garnish

4 garlic cloves, finely chopped

450-g/16-oz. can water chestnuts, drained and sliced

100 g/1 cup chopped peanuts

1 red chilli/chile, sliced, to garnish

SERVES 4–6

These hot and spicy Chinese chicken wings are sautéed in a pan for tender meat and a sweet and sticky sauce. Serve with other Chinese inspired bites for a fuller meal.

Combine 4 tablespoons of the wine, 4 tablespoons of the soy sauce, 2 tablespoons of the sesame oil and 4 tablespoons of the cornflour mixture in a bowl and mix together. Place the wings in a large, resealable plastic bag. Add the marinade, seal the bag and toss to coat. Place in the refrigerator to marinate overnight, or for at least 4 hours.

In a small bowl, combine the remaining wine, soy sauce, oil and cornflour mixture with the chilli paste, vinegar and sugar. Mix together and add the chopped onion, garlic, water chestnuts and peanuts. Transfer the mixture to a frying pan/skillet and heat the sauce slowly until aromatic.

Meanwhile, remove the chicken from the marinade and sauté in a second large frying pan until the meat is cooked through and the juices run clear when the thickest part is pierced to the bone. When the sauce is aromatic, add the sautéed chicken to it and let it simmer together until the sauce thickens, then serve immediately. Garnish with the sliced chilli and spring onion.

THAI GREEN CURRY WINGS

vegetable oil, for greasing

2 tbsp plain/all-purpose flour

2 tsp salt

2 tsp ground coriander

1.8 kg/4 lb. chicken wings, halved at the joints, tips removed

5 tbsp green chilli/chile sauce (either hot or mild, depending on your taste)

4 tbsp unsalted butter, melted

1 tbsp fish sauce

2 tsp Thai green curry paste

3 tbsp chopped fresh coriander/cilantro, to garnish

1 red chilli/chile, sliced, to garnish

COCONUT CREAM DIPPING SAUCE

400-g/16-oz. can coconut milk

225 g/1 cup brown sugar

SERVES 4–6

Of all the curries, Thai green curry seems to have the most flavour and aroma. Here, chicken wings are baked with a spicy green curry sauce.

First, make the dipping sauce. Combine the ingredients in a saucepan and bring to the boil over a medium-high heat. Reduce the heat to medium-low and cook, stirring, for about 20 minutes until the mixture is thick and the volume has reduced by about half. Set aside until needed.

Preheat the oven to 200°C (400°F) Gas 6. Line 2–3 baking sheets with foil and grease with vegetable oil.

In a bowl, mix the flour with the salt and ground coriander. Add the chicken and toss to coat. Spread the wings on the baking sheets in a single layer and drizzle with vegetable oil.

Roast in the preheated oven for 45 minutes, turning once or twice, until browned and crispy and the juices run clear when the thickest part is pierced to the bone.

In a bowl, whisk together the chilli sauce, butter, fish sauce and curry paste. Add the cooked chicken wings to the sauce and toss. Sprinkle with the chopped coriander and sliced chilli and serve with the dipping sauce on the side.

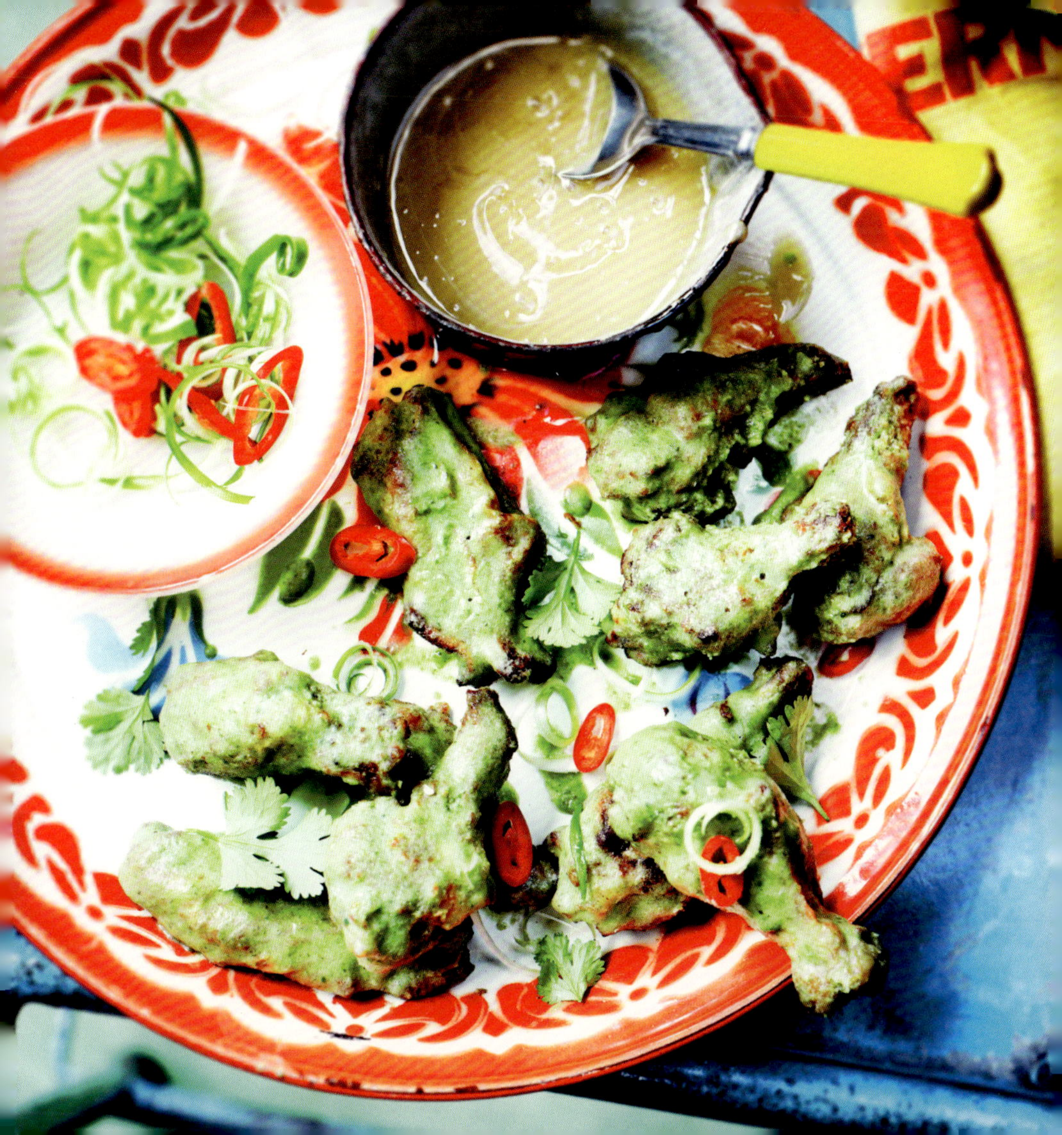

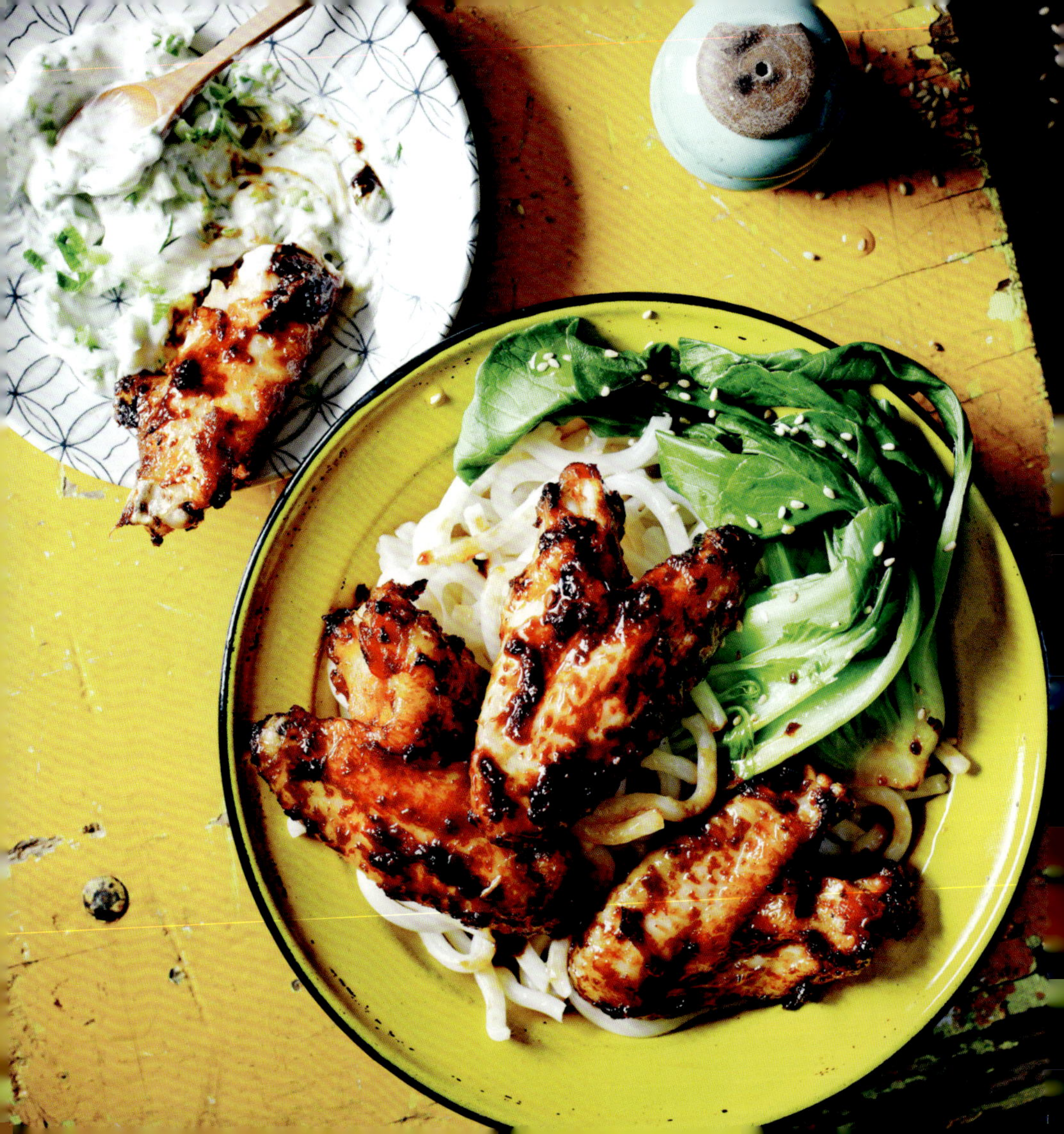

STICKY TERIYAKI WINGS

350 ml/1½ cups soy sauce

300 g/1½ cups sugar

175 ml/¾ cup pineapple juice

120 ml/½ cup vegetable oil

2 garlic cloves, finely chopped

1½ tbsp finely chopped fresh ginger

1.8 kg/4 lb. chicken wings, halved at the joints, tips removed

DIPPING SAUCE

225 ml/1 cup sour cream

225 g/1 cup mayonnaise

35 g/½ cup finely chopped spring onions/scallions

1 tbsp finely chopped flat-leaf parsley

1 garlic clove, finely chopped

1 tsp Dijon mustard

SERVES 4–6

These oven-baked teriyaki wings are marinated in a tangy pineapple-based teriyaki sauce and served with a tangy dipping sauce.

First make the dipping sauce by combining all the ingredients in a blender and whizzing until smooth. Transfer to a bowl, cover and chill until ready to serve.

Combine the soy sauce, sugar, pineapple juice, vegetable oil, garlic and ginger in a large bowl with 350 ml/1½ cups water. Stir until the sugar has dissolved. Pour the marinade into a large resealable plastic bag. Add the wings to the bag and marinate in the fridge overnight or for at least 4 hours.

Preheat the oven to 180°C (350°F) Gas 5. Line 2–3 baking sheets with foil.

Remove the chicken from the marinade and arrange on the baking sheets. Brush with the remaining marinade. Bake in the preheated oven for about 1 hour, or until the juices run clear when the thickest part is pierced to the bone.

Serve these wings with the dipping sauce for a tasty snack, or add cooked rice noodles and wilted Chinese cabbage/pak choi for a more substantial plateful.

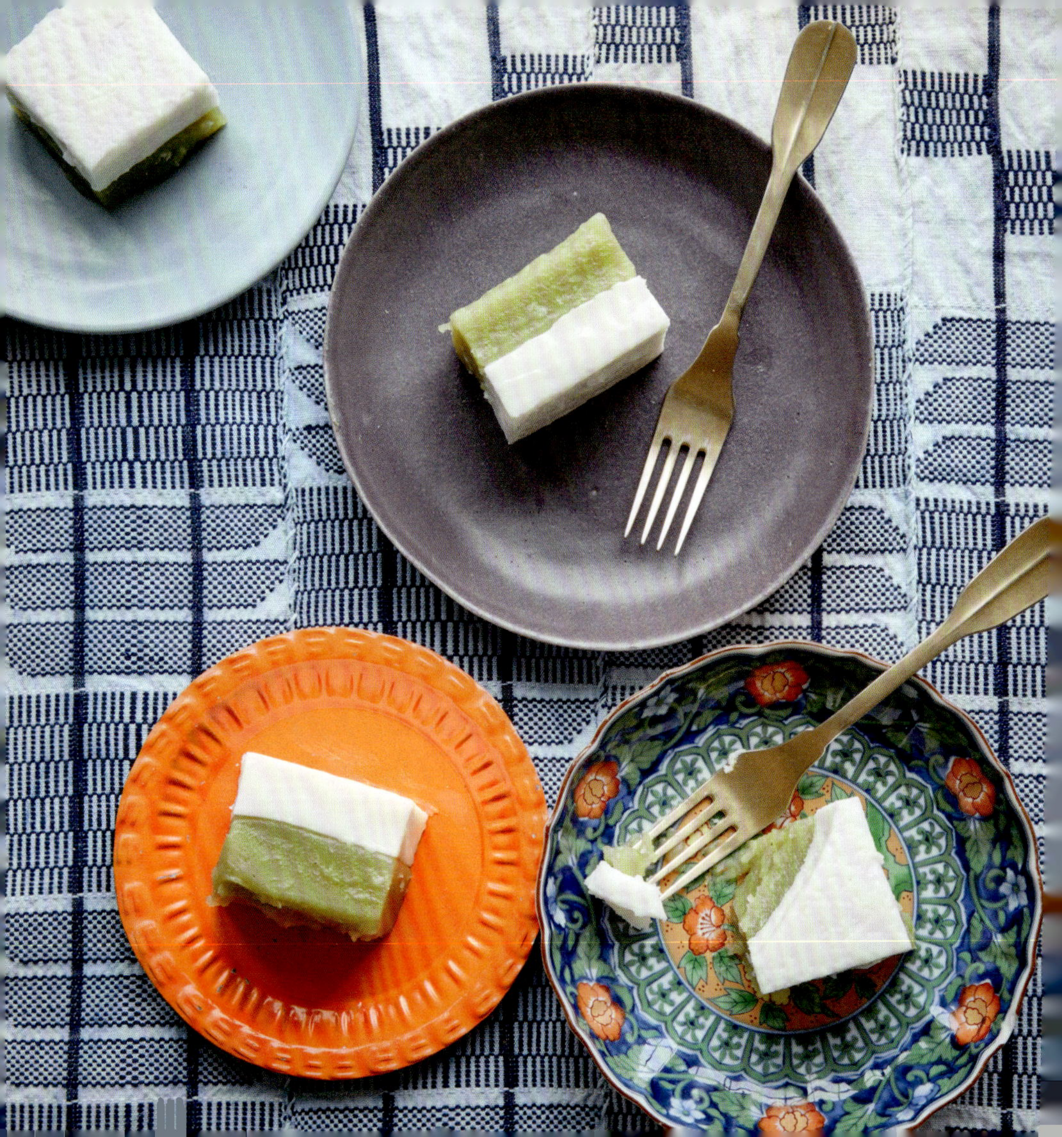

SWEET THINGS

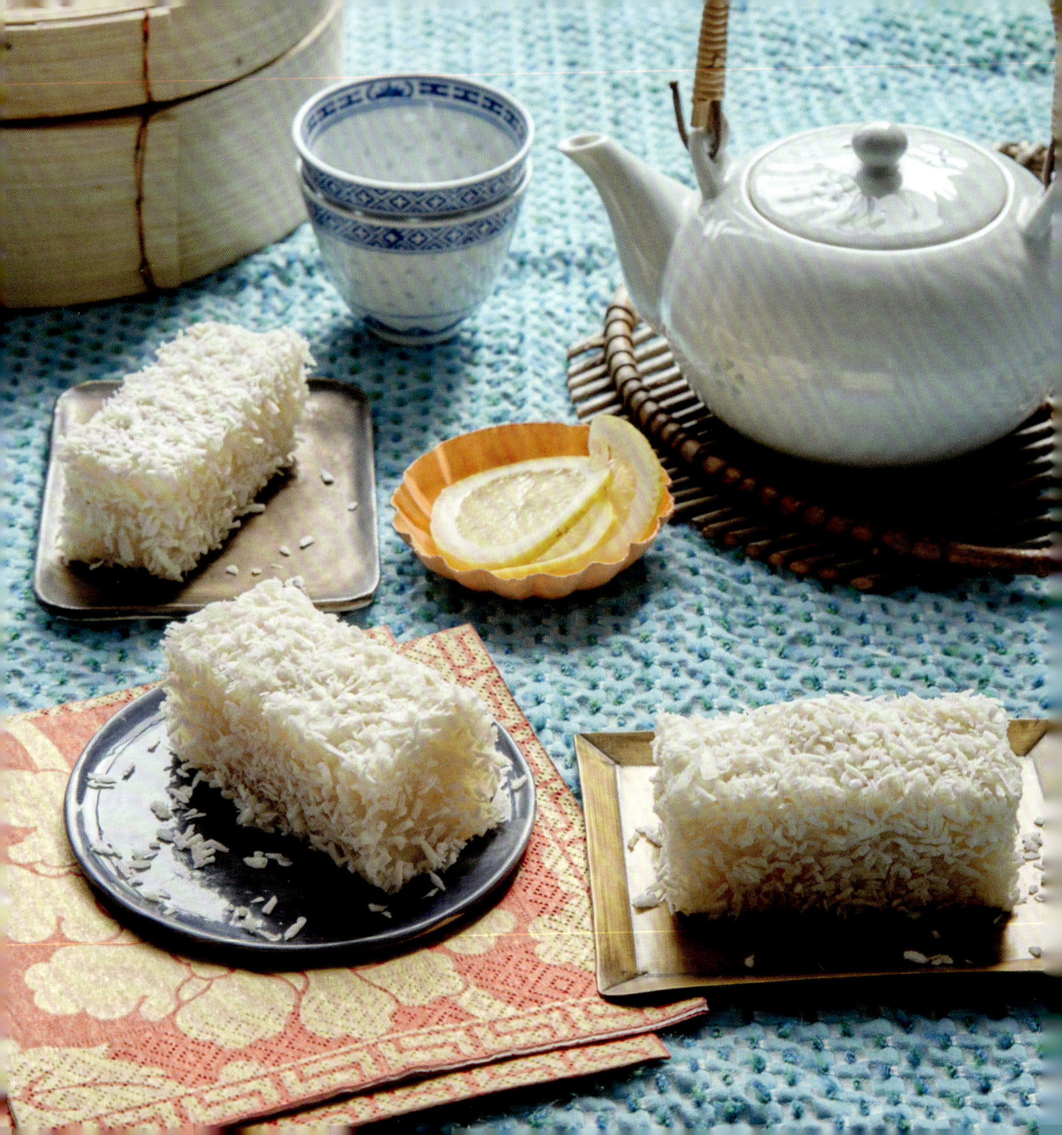

STEAMED CASSAVA CAKE

This Southeast-Asian-inspired sweet treat is very soft to eat and hardens in the fridge. It is traditionally eaten with a soft texture, but can be frozen and steamed to soften again when needed.

1 kg/2¼ lb. cassava

150 g/¾ cup white sugar

150 ml/⅔ cup coconut milk

8 pandan leaves, halved

1 tsp vegetable or sunflower oil

400 g/scant 6 cups grated coconut (you can buy it frozen or grate your own)

salt

steamer

2 x 26-cm/10¼-inch cake pans (or heatproof dishes), one lined with foil

MAKES 10–15

Peel and grate the cassava into a bowl and add 400 ml/scant 1¾ cups water, along with the sugar and coconut milk. Mix it evenly. Pour the mixture into the lined cake pans or heatproof dishes and spread the mixture out evenly. Arrange half the pandan leaves over the top, then place the pan in the steamer basket. Steam over boiling water for 40–45 minutes until set.

Place the remaining pandan leaves in the second (unlined) cake pan base. Mix ½ teaspoon salt into the grated coconut and put in the cake pan on top of the leaves. Steam the grated coconut over boiling water for 10 minutes (steaming helps to cook the coconut and stop it from going off too quickly). You can do this in a second tier steamer basket, if you like.

Remove the steamed cake and grated coconut from the steamer baskets. Remove and discard all the pandan leaves (they are used as aromatics only and are not to be eaten).

Using a spoon, shape the cake into bite-size pieces, or cut them into rectangles using a sharp knife. Coat each piece of cake with the steamed grated coconut.

MOCHI WITH ADZUKI RED BEAN FILLING

Mochi is a Japanese rice cake made from sticky rice flour. The cakes are very soft and chewy, and this version has a sweet-tasting homemade red bean paste filling made from dried adzuki beans.

100 g/¾ cup Thai, Japanese or Korean sticky rice flour

50 g/¼ cup unrefined sugar

about 250 g/2½ cups cornflour/cornstarch or potato starch, for dusting

FILLING

200 g/1 cup plus 2 tbsp dried adzuki red beans, soaked in water overnight

120 g/½ cup plus 2 tbsp white sugar

30 g/2½ tbsp soft brown sugar

salt

steamer

MAKES 12

For the filling, drain the adzuki red beans and discard the soaking liquid. Put the beans in a pan with 1 litre/4 cups water and bring to the boil. Simmer until softened; check after 1 hour, then again every 30 minutes until the beans are softened.

When the beans are soft, use a wooden spoon to stir in the sugars and 1 teaspoon salt. Continue to stir the beans in the pot until the mixture has almost become a dry paste (stir regularly or the beans can burn easily).

Pass the beans through a fine-mesh sieve/strainer to remove the skins, or you can just leave it as it is. Allow to cool and then cover and chill in the fridge for at least 2 hours.

Shape the red bean paste into 12 firm balls, then cover and chill again while you make the dough.

Whisk together the sticky rice flour and 150 ml/⅔ cup water in a bowl, then pour into a heatproof dish. Cover the dish with cling film/plastic wrap and place into the steamer basket. Steam over boiling water for 20 minutes, then remove from the steamer, add the sugar and stir with a wooden spoon until well combined.

Mochi dough is very sticky to work with, so generously dust the work surface and your hands with cornflour. Roll the mochi dough gently into a long sausage shape, then cut it into 12 portions. Roll each portion into a circle, dusting with cornflour as you go.

Remove the chilled bean paste balls from the fridge and place a ball on each circle of dough. Wrap the dough skin round the paste, sealing the seams. Turn the mochi seam-side down and shape it until round. Dust off excess any cornflour before enjoying as a tasty sweet snack.

SWEET THINGS

PANDAN & COCONUT LAYER CAKE

10 pandan leaves

20 g/¾ oz. mung bean starch

60 g/generous ½ cup tapioca starch

100 g/¾ cup rice flour

140 g/scant ¾ cup white sugar

½ tsp alkaline water

COCONUT MILK LAYER

50 g/generous ⅓ cup rice flour

25 g/1 oz. mung bean starch

280 ml/1 cup plus 2 tbsp thick coconut milk

250 ml/1 cup boiling water

salt

20-cm/8-inch semi-deep heatproof dish, lightly oiled

steamer

MAKES 12

This two-tone layer cake comprises a vibrant green pandan-infused base layer, topped with a brilliant white creamy coconut milk layer – delicious flavours of Southeast Asia and the perfect afternoon sweet snack. Alkaline water is available in large supermarkets.

Cut the pandan leaves into small pieces and put into a blender with 300 ml/1¼ cups water. Blend until you have pandan juice. Strain through a fine-mesh sieve/strainer to get 300 ml/1¼ cups pandan juice.

Put the mung bean starch, tapioca starch, rice flour and sugar in a bowl. Add the pandan juice, 350 ml/scant 1½ cups water and the alkaline water. Whisk until there are no lumps remaining.

Stain the mixture through a fine-mesh sieve/strainer into a saucepan and set it over a low heat to thicken slightly – it should coat the back of a wooden spoon lightly, do not over cook. Remove from the heat and pour the mixture into the base of the oiled heatproof dish.

Put the dish into the steamer basket and steam over boiling water for 15–20 minutes, or until the mixture is cooked and set.

To prepare the coconut milk layer, mix the rice flour, mung bean starch and 1 teaspoon salt in a heatproof bowl.

SWEET THINGS

Add the coconut milk. Gradually add the boiling water whilst whisking until the mixture is smooth. Strain if necessary to get rid of lumps.

Gently pour this layer over the green layer, then steam over boiling water (use a medium heat) for 15–17 minutes, or until the layer is set. It's important not to turn up the heat for this layer or the surface will not be smooth.

Allow the cake to cool completely, which may take an hour or so.

Rub a knife with some oil, or use a plastic knife, to cut the steam cake into small cubes. Wipe the knife with a damp cloth after each cut as the knife will be sticky.

SWEET THINGS **115**

MATCHA MOCHI WITH SWEET POTATO & PUMPKIN FILLING

Another tasty Japanese-inspired mochi recipe, but this time the chewy morsels are coloured green thanks to the matcha powder in the mochi dough, and they are filled with a vibrant orange-coloured sweet potato and pumpkin paste.

100 g/¾ cup Thai, Japanese or Korean sticky rice flour

5 g/1 tsp matcha powder

50 g/¼ cup unrefined sugar

about 250 g/2½ cups cornflour/cornstarch or potato starch, for dusting

FILLING

150 g/5¼ oz. sweet potato, peeled and chopped

100 g/3½ oz. pumpkin, peeled and chopped

25 g/2 tbsp caster/superfine sugar

2 tbsp sunflower or vegetable oil

50 g/5½ tbsp pumpkin seeds/pepitas, chopped

salt

steamer

MAKES 12

Start by making the filling. Arrange the sweet potato and pumpkin into a heatproof dish and place in the steamer basket. Steam over boiling water for about 20 minutes until softened.

Place the sweet potato and pumpkin into a blender and add the sugar, 60 ml/¼ cup water and a pinch of salt. Blend until smooth. Transfer the blended mixture into a frying pan/skillet and add the oil and the chopped pumpkin seeds. Cook over a low heat until the paste is firm. Allow the paste to cool and then cover and chill in the fridge for at least 2 hours.

Shape the pumpkin paste into 12 balls, then cover and chill again while you make the dough.

Whisk together the sticky rice flour, matcha powder and 150 ml/⅔ cup water in a bowl, then pour into a heatproof dish. Cover the dish with cling film/plastic wrap and place into the steamer basket. Steam over boiling water for 20 minutes, then remove from the steamer, add the sugar, and stir with a wooden spoon until well combined.

Mochi dough is very sticky to work with, so generously dust the work surface and your hands with cornflour. Roll the mochi dough gently into a long sausage shape, then cut it into 12 portions. Roll each portion into a circle, dusting with cornflour as you go.

Remove the chilled sweet potato and pumpkin paste balls from the fridge and place a ball on each circle of dough. Wrap the dough skin round the paste, sealing the seams. Turn the mochi seam-side down and shape it until round. Dust off excess cornflour before serving.

SWEET THINGS

DOSA BATTER CINNAMON WAFFLES
WITH DATE SYRUP

Dosa are thin savoury crêpes from India. Here the dosa batter has been re-imagined to make waffles. Soft, fluffy and as light as a cloud, these delightful waffles are served with a drizzle of reduced date syrup, which finishes this Indian-inspired dish off beautifully.

DOSA WAFFLE BATTER

150 g/5½ oz. dried split channa dhal, picked and rinsed, then soaked in 500 ml/ 2 cups lukewarm water overnight

150 g/5½ oz. basmati rice, soaked in 500 ml/ 2 cups cold water overnight

1 tbsp palm sugar/ jaggery

½ tsp ground cinnamon

½ tsp baking powder

DATE SYRUP

225 g/8 oz. soft stoned/ pitted dates

1 tsp palm sugar/ jaggery

200 ml/generous ¾ cup boiling water

waffle machine

SERVES 4 (MAKES 8 SMALL WAFFLES)

For the dosa batter, drain the channa dhal and basmati rice separately, retaining the soaking water from each separately, too.

Using a wet grinder if you have one (or a food processor), blitz the soaked channa dhal to a smooth purée, adding up to 10 spoonfuls of the soaking water gradually to help process it down. Set aside and then do the same with the soaked rice. It's better to grind them separately because the textures of the two grains can vary. Do not yet discard either of the remaining soaking waters.

Once blended, you should be left with around 270 g/9½ oz. ground

SWEET THINGS

rice purée and 460 g/1 lb. ground channa dhal purée. Combine both mixtures in a bowl and pour in 150 ml/⅔ cup of the remaining soaking water, from the rice or channa dhal. Add the palm sugar, cinnamon and baking powder and whisk together to form a batter similar in consistency to pancake batter. Set aside.

For the date syrup, combine the pitted dates, palm sugar and boiling water in a saucepan and simmer over a medium heat for 5–6 minutes, or until the dates are very soft. Use the wet grinder or food processor to blitz the dates with the excess liquid to form a syrup. Set aside.

To make the waffles, preheat the waffle machine following the manufacturer's instructions. Ladle in enough batter to cover the plate on one side (I use two small ladlefuls). Close the machine and cook for 12–15 minutes (cooking instructions do vary so check the instructions for your machine), then remove. Repeat for the remaining mixture; it should make 8 small waffles. Serve the warm waffles drizzled with the date syrup.

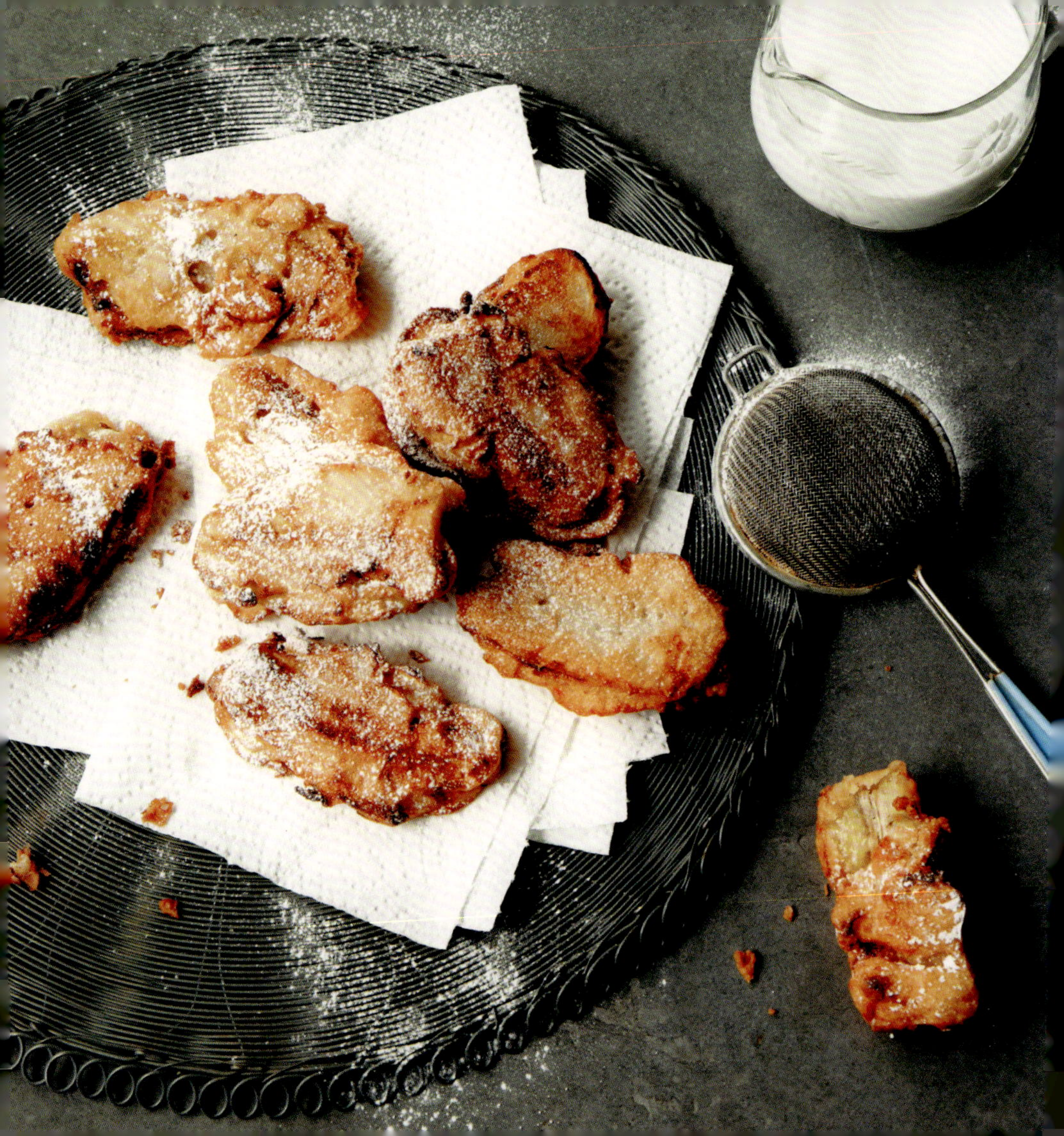

BANANA FRITTERS WITH COCONUT CUSTARD

Bananas are the most important traditional fruit of Vietnam. They are grown and sold everywhere and used in many dessert dishes. Just-ripe bananas work best with this recipe.

6 ripe bananas

200 g/1½ cups rice flour

1 x 400-ml.14-oz. can coconut milk

100 g/½ cup caster/granulated sugar

dash of pure vanilla extract or seeds from 1 vanilla pod/bean

4 tbsp sunflower/safflower oil

icing/confectioners' sugar, for dusting

COCONUT CUSTARD

1 x 400-ml/14-oz. can coconut milk

1 tsp salt

1 tsp caster/granulated sugar

SERVES 6–10

Slice the bananas in half lengthways, then cut them into 7.5-cm/3-inch pieces.

In a bowl, mix together the rice flour, coconut milk, sugar and vanilla to create a smooth batter. Add the bananas and mix to coat with batter.

Heat the oil in a frying pan/skillet over a medium heat and shallow fry the coated banana pieces for 2–3 minutes on each side or until golden brown. Set aside on paper towels.

To make the coconut custard, gently heat the coconut milk with the salt and sugar in a pan until warm.

Serve the fritters warm or at room temperature, dusted with icing sugar, with the coconut custard.

GAJJAR HALWA SAMOSAS

Samosas are a well-known Indian street food snack and 'Gajjar halwa' is carrot that has been simmered in sweetened milk until the milk has reduced down. These two Asian snacks have been combined to make a sweet filled samosa. Pistachio nuts and raisins are added for sweetness, colour and texture. The gajjar halwa acts as a fantastic filling as it is quite robust, which works well with the crispy fried pastry.

1 tbsp ghee

700 g/5¼ cups grated carrot

200 ml/¾ cup full-fat/whole milk

300 ml/1¼ cups condensed milk

a pinch of saffron strands

¼ tsp ground cardamom

1 tbsp caster/granulated sugar

4 tbsp (dark) raisins

5 tbsp chopped pistachio nuts

100 g/¾ cup plain/all-purpose flour

1 pack of filo/phyllo pastry (250 g/9 oz.)

ice cream, to serve

baking sheet, lined with baking parchment

SERVES 10 (MAKES 30 SAMOSAS)

Heat the ghee in a pan over a low heat and sauté the carrot for 20 minutes or until well softened.

Add the milk and reduce by half over low heat. This will take about 30 minutes, so be patient and keep stirring occasionally.

Add the condensed milk and saffron and simmer for a further 15 minutes. Add the ground cardamom, sugar, (dark) raisins and pistachio nuts and mix well.

Transfer to a shallow container and place in the refrigerator to cool and chill.

Meanwhile, prepare the flour glue by whisking the flour and 200 ml/¾ cup of water together.

Preheat the oven to 170°C (325°F) Gas 3.

Cut the filo sheets into 30 rectangles measuring 25 x 8 cm/10 x 3¼ inches. Keep the pastry covered until required.

When the filling has chilled, place roughly 30 g/1 oz. of filling at one end of a pastry rectangle. Take the right corner and fold diagonally to the left, enclosing the filling and forming a triangle. Fold again along the upper crease of the triangle. Keep folding this way until you are left with a little strip of pastry at the end.

Brush a little of the flour glue on the exposed bit of pastry, then fold over and enclose the samosa completely. Repeat to make 30 samosas.

Place all of the samosas on the prepared baking sheet and bake in the preheated oven for 15 minutes, turning them over after 5 minutes or so.

Serve the samosas warm with ice cream.

SWEET THINGS

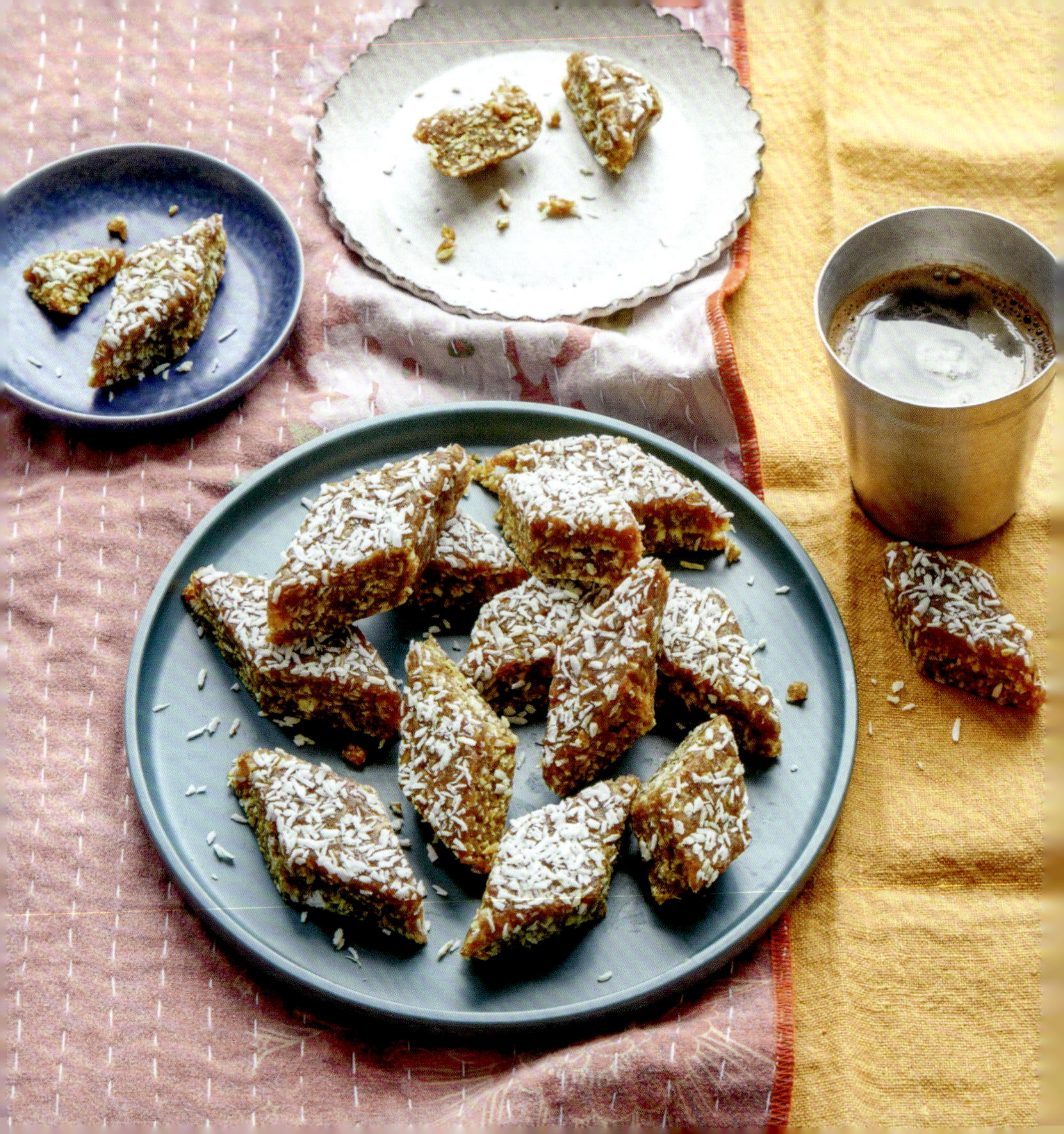

TURMERIC COCONUT BARFI

15 plump stoned/pitted dates

4 tbsp unsweetened oat or soya/soy milk

4-cm/1½-inch thumb of fresh turmeric, peeled, or use 1 tsp ground turmeric

1 tbsp extra-virgin coconut oil

45 g/scant ½ cup blanched ground almonds

70 g/scant 1 cup desiccated/dried unsweetened shredded coconut, plus 1 tbsp for sprinkling

1 scant tsp ground green cardamom seeds

20–25-cm/8–10-inch square baking pan, greased with extra-virgin coconut oil and base-lined with parchment

MAKES 16

Barfi is a popular Indian sweet snack. This adapted recipe uses dates with unsweetened oat milk to create a rich, sweet cream dessert.

Combine the dates, milk and fresh turmeric root (if using powder, add later) in a blender or food processor and blitz until you have a smooth paste.

Add the coconut oil to a small heavy-bottomed pan and place over a medium–high heat. Once the oil is fully melted, add the date purée. Bring to a simmer, then reduce the heat to low and cook gently for about 5–6 minutes, being careful not to burn it.

Next, add the blanched ground almonds, keeping the heat on low, and mix well to form a soft dough. Then add the coconut and cardamom (and ground turmeric, if using). Remove from the heat, and mix or knead until everything is evenly combined.

Press the mixture into the greased and lined baking pan, and, using the back of an oiled spoon, spread the mixture evenly until it is smooth. Sprinkle the extra 1 tablespoon coconut on the top, pressing down lightly. Chill for 1 hour in the fridge.

Remove from the pan by running a knife around the edge and carefully tipping it out onto a board. Cut into diamond or square shapes, and store in an airtight container in the fridge for up to 1 week.

INDEX

adzuki red beans: mochi 112–13
asparagus roll, miso-marinated 19
avocados: inside-out avocado rolls 20
vegan temaki rolls 52–3

banana fritters 121
bao buns: chicken teriyaki bao 34
dough 8–9
barbecue pork steamed buns 29
barfi, turmeric coconut 125
beef: beef bulgogi & rice noodle wraps 61
fiery beef satay 95
bhajis, courgette onion 76–7
bread: bread dough 8–9
fluffy bread dough 8
sesame prawn toasts 82–3
bulgogi: beef bulgogi & rice noodle wraps 61

cabbage: Chinese potstickers 38
Japanese okonomiyaki pancakes 64–5
cakes: pandan & coconut layer cake 114–15
steamed cassava cake 111
carrots: gajjar halwa samosas 122–3
pickled carrot 82–3
vegan temaki rolls 52–3
vegetarian spring rolls 58–9
cassava cake, steamed 111
channa dhal: channa dhal fritters 72–3
masala dhal vadas 90
chicken: chicken teriyaki bao 34

crispy chicken wontons 80
dumplings with makrut lime & lemongrass 37
kung pao wings 103
sticky teriyaki wings 107
Szechuan chicken steamed buns 30
Thai green curry wings 104
Thai-style fried chicken wings 100–1
yakitori-glazed mushroom & chicken skewers 99
Chinese dipping sauce 10
Chinese potstickers 38
choganjang 11
coconut: steamed cassava cake 111
turmeric coconut barfi 125
coconut cream dipping sauce 104
coconut milk: coconut custard 121
pandan & coconut layer cake 114–15
courgette/zucchini onion bhajis 76–7
crystal skin dough: salmon & mushroom dumplings 43
traditional prawn dumplings 40–1
cucumber: sashimi & cucumber bites 23
curry: Thai green curry wings 104
custard, coconut 121

dashi: Japanese dipping sauce 10
date syrup 118–19
dipping sauces: Chinese dipping sauce 10
coconut cream dipping sauce 104
hoisin & peanut dipping sauce 55

Japanese dipping sauce 10
Korean dipping sauces 11
lemongrass & soy dipping sauce 100–1
yogurt dip 89
dosa batter cinnamon waffles 118–19
dough: basic dough recipes 8
crystal skin dough 40–1
dressing, ginger soy 24
duck: duck satay with grilled pineapple & plum sauce 96
Peking-style duck pancake wraps 62–3
smoked duck rice paper rolls 55
dumplings: Chinese potstickers 38
dough 8
dumplings with makrut lime & lemongrass 37
kimchi noodle dumplings 44
salmon & mushroom dumplings 43
traditional prawn dumplings 40–1

eggs: egg dough 8
egg rolls 56–7

fermented seed pâté 52–3
fiery beef satay 95
filo/phyllo pastry: gajjar halwa samosas 122–3
fish: mixed sashimi 24
pickled salmon roll 16
salmon & mushroom dumplings 43
sashimi & cucumber bites 23
Thai fishcakes 79
wasabi mayonnaise & tuna roll 15
fritters: banana fritters 121
channa dhal fritters 72–3

gajjar halwa samosas 122–3
ginger soy dressing 24
gyoza wrappers: Chinese potstickers 38
kimchi noodle dumplings 44

hoisin & peanut dipping sauce 55

Indian vegetable pancakes 67
inside-out avocado rolls 20

Japanese dipping sauce 10
Japanese okonomiyaki pancakes 64–5

kakiage pancakes 74
kimchi noodle dumplings 44
Korean dipping sauces 11
Korean moong pancakes with pork 68–9
kung pao wings 103

lemongrass: dumplings with makrut lime & lemongrass 37
lemongrass & soy dipping sauce 100–1

makrut lime leaves: dumplings with makrut lime & lemongrass 37
mango: prawn & mango wontons 86
masala dhal vadas 90
mayonnaise: wasabi mayonnaise & tuna roll 15
miso-marinated asparagus roll 19
mochi 112–13
matcha mochi 116–17
moneybags, wonton pork 46–7
moong dal: Korean moong pancakes with pork 68–9

mushrooms: mushroom pakoras 89
salmon & mushroom dumplings 43
yakitori-glazed mushroom & chicken skewers 99

noodles: beef bulgogi & rice noodle wraps 61
prawns wrapped in noodles 85
smoked duck rice paper rolls 55
summer rolls 51
vegetarian spring rolls 58–9

okonomiyaki pancakes, Japanese 64–5
onion bhajis, courgette 76–7

pakoras, mushroom 89
pancakes: Indian vegetable pancakes 67
Japanese okonomiyaki pancakes 64–5
kakiage pancakes 74
Korean moong pancakes with pork 68–9
Peking-style duck pancake wraps 62–3
pandan & coconut layer cake 114–15
pâté, fermented seed 52–3
peanuts: hoisin & peanut dipping sauce 55
peanut sauce 95
Peking-style duck pancake wraps 62–3
pickles: pickled carrot 82–3
pickled salmon roll 16
pineapple: duck satay with grilled pineapple & plum sauce 96
pork: barbecue pork steamed buns 29
Chinese potstickers 38
egg rolls 56–7

kimchi noodle dumplings 44
Korean moong pancakes with pork 68–9
wonton pork moneybags 46–7
potatoes: masala dhal vadas 90
prawns/shrimp: fried prawn & scallop steamed buns 33
Japanese okonomiyaki pancakes 64–5
kimchi noodle dumplings 44
prawn & mango wontons 86
prawns wrapped in noodles 85
sesame prawn toasts 82–3
traditional prawn dumplings 40–1
wonton pork moneybags 46–7
pumpkin: matcha mochi 116–17
pumpkin seeds: fermented seed pâté 52–3

rice: inside-out avocado rolls 20
miso-marinated asparagus roll 19
pickled salmon roll 16
vinegared rice 9
wasabi mayonnaise & tuna roll 15
rice paper wrappers: smoked duck rice paper rolls 55
summer rolls 51

salmon: mixed sashimi 24
pickled salmon roll 16
salmon & mushroom dumplings 43
samosas, gajjar halwa 122–3
sashimi: mixed sashimi 24

sashimi & cucumber bites 23
satay: duck satay with grilled pineapple & plum sauce 96
fiery beef satay 95
sauerkraut: vegan temaki rolls 52–3
scallops: fried prawn/shrimp & scallop steamed buns 33
sesame prawn toasts 82–3
skewers: duck satay with grilled pineapple & plum sauce 96
fiery beef satay 95
yakitori-glazed mushroom & chicken skewers 99
smoked duck rice paper rolls 55
soy sauce: Chinese dipping sauce 10
ginger soy dressing 24
lemongrass & soy dipping sauce 100–1
spring rolls, vegetarian 58–9
ssamjang 11
steamed buns: barbecue pork steamed buns 29
fried prawn/shrimp & scallop steamed buns 33
Szechuan chicken steamed buns 30
steamed cassava cake 111
sticky teriyaki wings 107
sumac yogurt 76–7
summer rolls 51
sushi: inside-out avocado rolls 20
miso-marinated asparagus roll 19
pickled salmon roll 16
wasabi mayonnaise & tuna roll 15
sweet & sour sauce 56–7
sweet potatoes: matcha mochi 116–17

Szechuan chicken steamed buns 30

temaki rolls, vegan 52–3
teriyaki: chicken teriyaki bao 34
sticky teriyaki wings 107
Thai fishcakes 79
Thai green curry wings 104
Thai-style fried chicken wings 100–1
tuna: mixed sashimi 24
sashimi & cucumber bites 23
wasabi mayonnaise & tuna roll 15
turmeric coconut barfi 125

vadas, masala dhal 90
vegan temaki rolls 52–3
vegetables: Indian vegetable pancakes 67
vegetarian spring rolls 58–9
vinegared rice 9

waffles, dosa batter cinnamon 118–19
wasabi mayonnaise & tuna roll 15
water chestnuts: kung pao wings 103
wontons: crispy chicken wontons 80
prawn & mango wontons 86
wonton pork moneybags 46–7
wraps: beef bulgogi & rice noodle wraps 61
Peking-style duck pancake wraps 62–3

yakitori-glazed mushroom & chicken skewers 99
yogurt: sumac yogurt 76–7
yogurt dip 89

INDEX **127**

RECIPE CREDITS

Ghillie Başan
Duck Satay
Fiery Beef Satay

Jordan Bourke
Courgette & Onion Bhajis
Japanese Okonomiyaki Pancakes

James Campbell
Kakiage Pancakes

Ross Dobson
Sesame Prawn Toasts

Matt Follas
Thai Fishcakes

Dunja Gulin
Vegan Temaki Rolls with Seed Pâté

Tori Haschka
Sashimi & Cucumber Bites

Carol Hilker
Egg Rolls
Kung Pao Wings
Sticky Teriyaki Wings
Summer Rolls
Thai Green Curry Wings
Thai-style Fried Chicken Wings

Vicky Jones
Korean Moong Pancakes

Jackie Kearney
Indian Vegetable Pancakes
Turmeric Coconut Barfi

Jenny Linford
Crispy Chicken Wontons
Mushroom Pakoras
Yakitori Chicken & Mushroom Skewers

Loretta Liu
Barbecue Pork Steamed Buns
Clamshell Bao with Chicken Teriyaki
Fried Shrimp & Scallop Bao
Kimchi Noodle Dumplings
Little Szechuan Chicken Steamed Buns
Matcha Mochi
Mochi with Adzuki Red Bean Filling
Pandan & Coconut Layer Cake
Salmon & Mushroom Dumplings
Shrimp & Mango Wontons
Steamed Cassava Cake
Traditional Prawn Dumplings

Uyen Luu
Banana Fritters

Nitisha Patel
Channa Dhal Fritters
Dosa Batter Cinnamon Waffles with Date Syrup
Gajar Halwa Samosas
Masala Dhal Vadas

Elsa Petersen-Schepelern
Wonton Pork Moneybags

Louise Pickford
Beef Bulgogi & Rice Noodle Wraps
Chinese Dipping Sauce
Chinese Potstickers
Dumplings with Makrut Lime & Lemongrass
Japanese Dipping Sauce
Korean Dipping Sauces
Prawns Wrapped in Noodles
Smoked Duck Summer Rolls
Vegetarian Spring Rolls

Annie Rigg
Mixed Sashimi

Fiona Smith
Inside-out Avocado Rolls
Miso-marinated Asparagus Roll
Peking-style Duck Pancake Wraps
Pickled Salmon Roll
Wasabi Mayo & Tuna Roll

PHOTOGRAPHY CREDITS

Steve Baxter
Page 25.

Peter Cassidy
Pages 57, 92, 101, 102, 105, 106.

Tara Fisher
Pages 65, 70, 77.

Louise Hagger
Pages 26, 28, 32, 41, 42, 87.

Richard Jung
Page 97.

Mowie Kay
Page 74.

Diana Miller
Pages 12, 14, 16, 18, 21.

Steve Painter
Pages 2, 78.

William Reavell
Page 69.

Toby Scott
Page 53.

Ian Wallace
Pages 3, 5, 6, 39, 45, 54, 59, 60, 84, 94.

Isobel Weld
Page 22.

Kate Whittaker
Page 83.

Clare Winfield
Pages 1, 31, 35, 36, 47, 48, 50, 63, 66, 73, 81, 88, 91, 98, 108, 110, 113, 115, 117, 119, 120, 123, 124.